Samadhi

The Superconsciousness
of the Future

MOUNI SADHU

VIVEKA CHUDAMANI by Sankaracharya

Verse 37: '*Salutation to thee, O Lord, full of compassion, O friend of those who bend before thee. I have fallen into the ocean of birth and rebirth. Rescue me by thy never failing glance which rains the ambrosia of sincerity and mercy.*'

Verse 38: '*Protect from death him who is heated by the roaring wild fire of changing life so difficult to extinguish, him who is oppressed and buffeted by the blasts of misfortune, since no other refuge do I know.*'

Mandala Books
UNWIN PAPERBACKS
London   Boston   Sydney

First published in Great Britain by
George Allen and Unwin 1962
Reprinted 1971
First published in Unwin Paperbacks 1976
Reissued 1980

UNWIN® PAPERBACKS
40 Museum Street, London WC1A 1LU

© Mouni Sadhu 1962, 1976

ISBN 0 04 149039 8

Reproduced, printed and bound
in Great Britain by
Hazell Watson & Viney Ltd,
Aylesbury, Bucks

Samadhi means 'superconsciousness'. Writing directly from his own experience, Mouni Sadhu, the well-known author of *The Tarot*, *Concentration*, *Meditation* and *In Days of Great Peace*, demonstrates the way to develop a keener sense of awareness, the means of transcending the dichotomy between body and mind and the method of achieving a lasting sense of spirituality and inner peace. Based on the methods of the author's own spiritual mentor, Ramana Maharshi, *Samadhi* is a practical manual leading to clear and scientific conceptions about the different forms of consciousness.

Contents

DEDICATION

*'To the Light which illumines
every man who comes into the World'*

The verses which have been inserted at the beginning
of each chapter are taken from Sri Sankaracharya's
Viveka Chudamani (The Crest Jewel of Wisdom) translated by Mohini M. Chatterji, 1898.

PART I

Preliminaries

Chapter I

Definition of Samadhi and Its Aims

Verse 6: 'He may study the scriptures, propitiate the gods (by sacrifices), perform religious ceremonies or offer devotion to the gods, yet he will not attain salvation even during the succession of a hundred Brahma-yugas except by the knowledge of union with the spirit.'

IN the second half of the twentieth century, the question of the higher aspects of consciousness in man, often called simply the *Superconsciousness*, is becoming more and more urgent for deeply thinking people. Many works have appeared on the subject, and from their popularity one can judge of the interest connected with it.

But it is not easy to find a practical manual which leads to clear and scientific conceptions about the different forms of the Superconsciousness, which in the East is called Samadhi. It is even more difficult to find authors who do not merely write compilations from the classical works of the Indian Initiates, but who speak from their own firsthand experience. Such experience alone can become a living truth for eager and earnest students, who feel a strong desire to attain the peaks, about which they can find many incomparable treatises in Eastern philosophical literature, such as the Vedas, the Upanishads, the works of Sankaracharya, Ashtavakra and finally of the modern Great Rishi of India—Ramana Maharshi.

For a thinking man, there is no doubt that consciousness in human beings is subjected to a steady evolution. Nobody would deny that even a couple of thousand years ago the *Self* in man was much more primitive than in this twentieth century, not to mention prehistoric races and tribes, belonging to, say, the Stone Age, and so on.

Despite the fact that humanity is undergoing the evolution of its inner treasure, that is Self-consciousness, it does not follow that everyone is progressing at the same rate. In this matter there is not, and never has been, any equality. The paths were always shown by the most advanced sons of man, and the rest followed, more or less slowly. There is no doubt that were a Socrates or a Pythagoras living in our own time, they would also be recognized as sages and eminent men, at least, by those whose inner criterion is sufficiently advanced.

But this does not mean that *all* people living in Socrates' time would find similar recognition and respect because of their qualities, which, to us, might well appear to be somewhat limited and primitive.

And so it is with our own period : a few people become ripe enough to tread new paths, as, for example, the one which forms the subject of this book, and which treats of the 'new' forms of consciousness in us. The masses are not yet interested in these, preferring to use the more material aspects of civilization, such as the latest in technical progress, with all the accompanying inventions and gadgets.

This book, like my former ones, has not been written in order to expound some 'new' theories as teachings. There are enough in existence, which, if followed, bring the aspirant to the individual knowledge of the Truth of his (and everyone's) being.

Here you will find advice on how to proceed on the Path, and how to get first-hand experience of that which, so far, for the overwhelming majority of humans, remains as only a misty picture of unreality.

My aim here is not to provide any additional mental knowledge, but to aid in the development of the higher consciousness, which alone reveals the ultimate Truth, which is the final goal of everything.

I mentioned a 'new' type of consciousness, a wider and brighter one, in two former books, which form the first and second parts of my mystic trilogy, being respectively : *In Days of Great Peace* and *Concentration*. An extensive study of both these books is necessary before one can attempt to make a start with the present work, which is the culminating point for its two predecessors. *In Days of Great Peace* deals with the experiences leading to the enlargement of consciousness, while *Concentration* gives the necessary explanations and techniques for the first step, that is, domination of one's own mind.

This book speaks about the ultimate aim, the achievement of the Superconsciousness—Samadhi, and the ways leading to it.

*   *   *   *

As a principal definition, according to the Eastern and Western occult tradition, we have to make a strict distinction between two kinds of terms :

(1) *Supersensual Visions, Ecstasies, Apparitions, Magic Evocations, Sixth Sense* and *Mesmeric* and *Spiritist Phenomena*, briefly, all those things which we know from popular books on occult themes, and

(2) *True Superconsciousness, independent of all visions and other inner or outer conditions* in which man can find himself.

14

This distinction between terms is an axiom, given to us by those who know.

These two kinds of terms (1) and (2) will become well understood when we rightly analyse what all these visions and ecstasies actually are. In this book I shall call as foremost evidence and authority for the Eastern spiritual philosophy, the sayings of the latest Great Rishi of India, Sri Ramana Maharshi (1879-1950).

This is because he was the leading contemporary exponent of Indian philosophical thought, and because he lived in our own period and was able to adapt, explain and deepen that thought for us. As considerable literature already exists about this spiritual giant, I will refrain from giving many particulars about his biography and teachings, since both can easily be found in other books about Sri Maharshi (see also *In Days of Great Peace*).

So, we will call the aforementioned enlargements of perception (visions, ecstasies, trances, clairvoyance, clairaudience, mediumism, and so on), just the sharpening and developing of the other than physical senses in man, but which are still only a different kind of activity of those senses. So taught the Maharshi himself. Consequently we see that in this case no principle has been changed, only the scale of perceptions has become wider. In other words, there still remains the old *binary*: I and Non-I. In occult philosophy, unsolved binaries are known as unproductive conceptions, which keep us in the old basic ignorance of the ultimate Truth of Being.

Therefore, we cannot have any hope in such a dualistic condition. No matter how apparently sublime and beautiful the extension of our means of cognition might be for us, when directed outwards, that is, to the so-called *Non-I*, there will always remain the unbroken relativity, just like the unpleasant, bitter spoon of tar, hidden at the bottom of a barrel of pure honey, which spoils the contents, because we must inevitably reach it. Therefore, in the relativity of our merging into different worlds (not only the physical one, of course, but also in those of more subtle matter, of which we will speak extensively in Chapter III), there cannot be found any ultimate, that is absolute and not relative consciousness, which alone can be defined as true 'Superconsciousness'.

I hope all of this sufficiently explains the first kind of terms as given previously in (1). At the same time, the second now becomes justified and understandable, and with it, the whole conception of *Samadhi*. We will reject the use of this expression for all the phenomena from (1), which some insufficiently knowledgeable exponents call the '*lower kinds of Samadhi*'. From our point of view there is only *one* Samadhi, without any relation to the manifested worlds, and there-

fore it is independent, above and beyond all time and space, the ultimate, absolute, unchangeable *Reality*, our final inheritance and
eternal rest.

It may be advisable here to quote two important statements of the
Maharshi, who, in his usually concise and direct manner says:

(a) *Samadhi alone can reveal the truth.*

(b) *In Samadhi there is only the feeling of I-I, and no thoughts.*

The first statement (a) does not need any further explanation now
that we have analysed the first kind of term; but the second statement
(b) is evidently an effort to express in the mind's language and terminology, what actually cannot be interpreted in any words. Even
under such a difficulty this saying of the Sage Maharshi has a
highly enlightening and practical character, for it is a direct answer
to the question:

'What is there in Samadhi, when man is in that state of consciousness?'

Evidently, it is the basic, glorious *Oneness*, without any more
duality. There is only the wordless and thoughtless *I*, or *I am*. In-
cidentally, that *I am that I am* is a definition of the Supreme Being
(Essence), as given to us in the Old Testament. The Maharshi more
than once underlined this fact.

The aim to be reached through the attainment of Samadhi is to
enter into a state of *pure consciousness*, in which there is no subject
nor object. There is no need to point out that such a state is far beyond all incarnations, that is life in forms; it actually transcends all
bodies, limitations and conditions, in which there is no subject nor
object, as was said previously. Admittedly, it is not easy even to
imagine such heights through our mind's efforts; but this is only
natural and logical. In Samadhi the mind is left far below, as an
instrument of consciousness, and with it fall away all feelings and
thoughts, which are absent in that sublime state. All changes also
cease.

The *Peace* alone remains which cannot be disturbed by anything.
This is the peace, which surpasses all human understanding (mind).
And yet, even now, there are souls on this Earth, who have reached
that *Peace*, and also those who are still struggling to reach it. They
will fully understand the meaning of this chapter.

Chapter II

Development of the Subtle Senses and the Superconsciousness in Man

Verse 8: 'Therefore the wise man strives for his salvation. having renounced his desire for the enjoyment of external objects, and betakes himself to a true and great teacher and accepts his teaching with an unshaken soul.'

IN his relations with the outer world, a very average man uses only his five physical senses, for his world does not extend beyond the limits of matter. To him it seems to be the only natural and understandable way of life. When he strikes, say, his toe against a stone, it is *himself* who was struck, and he who consequently suffers. A hearty meal and a drink, for example, bring enjoyment to just *himself*. Praise addressed to his visible form, as well as criticism, both necessarily affect that which such a man considers to be himself. For some of my readers, this point might seem to be exaggerated; but please, make a practical test for yourself.

Try to retain full serenity in your mind when being insulted; when told about considerable material losses, or a dangerous disease, which is developing in your body. If you can do so, then it will be proof that there is something above the 'normal' consciousness in you. Check on this.

Imagine that you are returning from a consultation with a specialist, because of a persistent pain in some part of your body. He did not give you any outright diagnosis of your ailment, but spoke of the necessity for further tests, and so on. Next day you might see distress on the faces of your relatives, your wife or husband, who knew about your visit and had been informed of its results by the doctor.

Then, you may recognize the truth in their anxious expressions, and finally, you learn it for yourself, that your days or months are numbered. Would you not be deeply shocked, distressed, perhaps in despair, so firmly bound are you to this physical plane? But someone can say: 'Apart from the physical consciousness we are still living in a world of emotions, feelings and thoughts, which no less affect us than purely material circumstances.' Well, that is so, but unfortunately, even these are closely connected with the physical events of your everyday life, and cannot possibly be completely separated from it.

In the instinctive, uncontrolled belief that we are our bodies lies the cause of our slavery to the physical world. For then we cannot detach ourselves and look on our body as on an object, somewhat apart from 'ourselves'. One day we may enter into contact with people who believe in some 'subtler' senses, abilities and worlds, that they have experienced only on the physical level. Occultists, spiritists, different odd sects, and so on, try to extend the limits of their cognition beyond the dense matter to which the five senses are subjected. They speak about other kinds of vibrations, accessible to those who develop the so-called 'sixth sense', and so on.

There is some relative truth in all of this. By special exercises, diet, way of life, breath control and research it is possible to widen the field of our perceptions (see *Concentration* Parts I and II) and to experience many of the theoretical statements made in occult books.

Clairvoyance, clairaudience, and visions coming from the 'other world' are not necessarily fantasies and inaccessible experiences, despite their elusiveness and the uncertainty of their origin. Often our own imagination and autosuggestion play the major roles in our 'experiences on the other side'. Only very learned occultists who have great stamina and who have had extensive practice in their search, along with the resulting knowledge, can be taken into consideration. Even then, amazing errors can happen. Visions in the supersensual worlds (I mean physical senses) are too individual and confused to be confirmed as being infallible. That is why occult masters place such weight on the proper training of the astral and higher senses in their pupils, teaching them to see things just as they themselves do.

Some forty years ago (I am writing this in 1960), leaders of a world wide society, in their books and lectures, proclaimed the coming of a new *messiah*, whom they declared to have been prepared by themselves for that sublime role. They spoke about their astral investigations, which unmistakably showed the person of the new teacher and his high spiritual powers. In some countries people began to deify him in advance, even building vast stadiums for his preaching.

And the end? The *messiah* flatly repudiated his role and left the whole organization, thereby creating bitter confusion and disappointment. The prophecies and visions were wrong.

*   *   *   *

Coming back to the methods of development of the occult powers in man (called *siddhis* in the East), I will limit myself to only a brief enumeration, as the aim of this work is the study of the Superconsciousness, and not the lower kinds of development, called 'psychic'.

The foremost means are: *mental concentration*, leading to domination of one's mind and its processes; *breathing exercises*, helping to dominate the prana or vital, subtle energy, thus enabling us to act on the astral plane; *fasts* which strengthen our will-power and purify the body; the *use of drugs*, which is forbidden in 'white' schools; *incantations and mantras*, being another form of concentration, connected with the use of the power inherent in sounds, and many other means, which are not openly known, and therefore cannot be mentioned.

These means may help in the development of some subtle senses, somewhat in advance of those of the present human race, and so enable us to peep into other worlds. But does this mean any attainment of the higher consciousness, to say nothing of the Superconsciousness, that is Samadhi? For then a man still remains essentially the same. If he was ego-centred before, say, his attainment of the astral sight, he will still be the same afterwards, no matter even if he can see elementals, human phantoms and other details of the world, normally hidden from human perception.

Such a man can still be easily frightened by physical death, which means that he prefers the physical existence to every other form of life.

No, the way to the Superconsciousness evidently does not lie in that direction. As support of this, I will mention only that the Maharshi referred to all the occult phenomena, which we previously spoke about, as being the play of man's own mind, which has no objective reality. Under the term mind, the Sage understood all superphysical manifestations, including siddhis (occult powers).

Christian saints also denied any importance to similar phenomena (see *Concentration*, Part II).

On the other hand the development of Samadhi, as we will see in the following chapters, changes the whole consciousness of a man, his point of view, his interests, strivings and aims. It kills the ego-centred attitude, and shows him the physical life as it really is, in all its relativity and imperfections. It removes the phantom of death, which is inseparable from existence in a body. Then man does not consider himself as a cumbersome, theoretical combination of 'body and soul', of course, having no real knowledge of the latter, but operating only with borrowed theorizing.

No, in attainment of the *Absolute Consciousness* (in Samadhi) there is no room for any relativity or imperfections. The very term

19

(Samadhi) presupposes the surpassing of all things subjected to time and space. It is worth thinking deeper about this last sentence, if we want to form even a right mental conception of the Superconsciousness. There is nothing more to be attained when the *Fourth State*, as the Maharshi calls it, is reached (see *Concentration*, Part II, Chapter XIII).

Is it possible? I have my own personal proof of it. When I saw the Master I knew that he was the living example of true Attainment, and in his presence no doubt could arise any more about the possibility of that Attainment. This certainly was independent of all books and theories on the subject.

In our inner development in the direction of the Superconsciousness nothing avails, with the exception of our own unmistakable experience. For, only then do we *know*, and not merely repeat some foreign words, which are then dead letters and little more.

My old friend, the late Swami Siddheswarananda of Paris, who spent almost twenty years in that city, and who was head of the Ramakrishna Mission in France, once remarked:

'In our spiritual work (in which the striving for true Superconsciousness is foremost) we should not accept any statement, heard or read, without an inner examination. A prior process in our consciousness is necessary, a process which awakens intellectual intuition in us. One should not merely repeat: Ramakrishna said this, Maharshi said that, and the Swami said something else. We should not incessantly quote an authority, which may serve us merely as a refuge. It is a great obstacle to all progress if one is seeking only such an imaginary refuge, instead of working arduously oneself. Enlightenment must come from within ourselves, that is from our own Atman, awakened by our own efforts and pain. Words, lectures of a Swami, the reading of a text from Ramakrishna's teachings, and so on, can only be external means, which produce an inner inquiry. This analysis within oneself is absolutely necessary. A lecture on the Gita or Upanishads is only an opportunity for the awakening in us of spiritual intelligence (Buddhi). We should reach the state of being dissatisfied, because if we take rest and remain satisfied, no progress will be possible.' (Translated from the French.)

This quotation may show us the attitude of those who reached Samadhi for themselves and who know it from experience.

Chapter III

Occult Theories about the Higher Worlds

Verse 11: 'Actions are for the purification of the heart, not for the attainment of the real substance. The substance can be attained by right discrimination, but not by any amount of Karma.'

IN order to elucidate, as much as possible, the hard problem concerning true Samadhi and its attainment, we have to become acquainted with the theories of the higher (that is, less material) worlds, in which our consciousness is able to function, under certain special conditions. In our present study we cannot avoid being confronted with non-material powers which affect our normal consciousness (that is, our everyday one).

These are: our feelings and emotions (called astral) and thoughts (called mental processes). We cannot *see* them but they exist and function. The average man, who does not possess any power of discrimination, which would allow him to analyse himself, combines together everything in his physical form and life. We cannot be satisfied with such simplicity, because it does not allow us to proceed any further in our study.

Therefore, it is supposed, as an acceptable working theory, that every manifestation must have at least *two* elements: the *acting* force and the *surroundings* or *screen* in, or on which, that force manifests itself. There is no doubt that our emotions and thoughts are *forces*, which often appear as very powerful factors in our lives. They can even kill or resuscitate. Therefore, there should be some kind of suitable matter in which these universal forces can act.

So arose the occult conception of the astral (feelings and emotions) and mental (thoughts and ideas) planes or worlds. We encounter them in the oldest recorded occultism, reaching back into the days of the ancient Egyptians, Chaldeans, Hindus, Persians and also the Greeks, who borrowed these ideas from the East.

Here I will briefly describe both of these worlds, invisible to the physical eye. As can be deduced from previous remarks, the astral plane (world) penetrates the physical one. This is possible because astral atoms are infinitely more subtle and smaller than the physical. Official science tells us that an atom is just like a miniature solar system, in which its planets (electrons satellites) circle at enormous speed around the central body (nucleus), which is like the sun. But they never touch and the distances between them are still greater (relatively) than those between the sun and its satellites like the Earth, and so on.

It is because of the infinitely large distances between the elements of the atoms and also the atoms themselves, belonging to the physical world, that other worlds endowed with different degrees of density in their substance can easily be 'inserted' into it.

The word 'inserted' is, of course, inadequate, for there is still the conception of the next (in this case, fourth) dimension, but for the sake of simplicity we may accept this definition.

Anyway, this idea does not contradict the actual conditions regarding the different kinds of matter belonging to the different planes of existence. So the astral (emotional) world (1) does interpenetrate, but (2) also transcends the physical plane of three dimensions, as it possesses the *fourth* dimension, related to the third just as the *third* is to the second. If we grasp this idea, then the phenomena of the astral world will find their logical explanation. It should be added, that the reader must not follow the theories of some thinker-mathematicians of the beginning of this century, who supposed that the fourth (imaginary for our minds) co-ordinate (added to the three co-ordinates officially used in trigonometry) is *just that of time*!

It is not so, because, although time still exists in the higher planes, in them it has quite a different meaning, and cannot be fully compared with *earthly time*. St Peter the Apostle in his Second Epistle tells us about an amazing fact, that: '. . . *one day with the Lord is as a thousand years, and a thousand years as one day.*'

This is an interesting and successful attempt to describe in human language (that of the three dimensions) the conditions reigning in the higher worlds. In the astro-mental (that is, still material) worlds, the clichés of the three sub-divisions of our time (that is the past, present and future) have no separate meaning. Deep thought about the foregoing might give you a right and realistic conception of the 'superior kind of time' existing in the higher, less dense worlds.

Now you may realize why, for example, in our dreams we are sometimes able to live a long period of experiences, apparently extending for years, but which in fact take us only a few minutes of 'earthly' time. These cases are too well known and many of my readers have certainly experienced this phenomenon personally, apart from the numerous descriptions which can be found in many psychological and occult books, so there is no need to quote many examples. When awakening during the night one notes the time, then falls asleep again and has a dream which depicts several years of one's life, so that details are perfectly recorded in the dreamer's memory. Yet, a glance at the clock on the bedside table shows that sleep has lasted only a few minutes, usually less than a quarter of an hour.

In dreams we apparently visit far-off countries, sometimes thousands of miles apart, and from these 'dreamy' travels we often bring back very clear remembrances recorded in the brain's memory. Occultists term these experiences 'astral journeys'. Again, in the astral plane, as we can see, the means of communication are far more effective, from the point of view of speed, than in the three-plane physical world. I know that there are many people, who deny all value to the experiences just described, as well as of the existence of any 'higher' worlds.

Unfortunately, these people cannot bring forward, or offer any logical and reasonable theory in order to explain the phenomena of inner life to those who have been confronted by these phenomena. But the same people will also deny all that we say here about the superior states of consciousness, leading to Samadhi, as well as Samadhi itself. Naturally, I have nothing to say to men, who are unable to offer us anything better than stark negations. But the title of this chapter is clear : it speaks about the *theories* which occultism offers, in order to explain phenomena which otherwise cannot be explained. No scientist ever saw an atom, to say nothing of the infinitesimal components of one. And yet, the atomic theory works and is accepted, and even brings quite real proofs of its truthfulness, in the form of hundreds of thousands of victims in two annihilated cities fifteen years ago, plus the actual poisoning of the earthly atmosphere by nuclear tests, to give a foretaste of future developments.

And so it is with the approaches to Samadhi. We must have reasonable and workable explanations along the paths which lead to the final target, transcending all worlds and matter, the physical (well known to us, as we believe) and all the theoretical ones, about which occultism teaches.

To resume, the first 'higher' world above the physical is that of emotions and feelings, and is called the *astral*. When we have to experience these two (that is, emotions and feelings), the subtle matter of the astral plane begins to vibrate in tune with the motive force, which provides the impulse. In our case (I am speaking here about human activities in the astral world) this force moulds forms and currents in the astral corresponding to the ideas created by men themselves, and its name is—*will-power*. Here there will possibly be protests on the part of some of my readers. 'I never wanted certain feelings to arise in me,' they may say. 'The feelings and emotions which followed were painful and undesirable. And yet, in spite of all that, I had them to my own detriment. Of that I am sure.'

At first glance there may be some reason in such an attitude; but let us look better and deeper, and then we will see something different. The astral world is full of vortexes and currents of every kind, just as the ocean is full of fish, animals, plants and currents. When we are fishing we usually do not know exactly what fish we will catch at a given moment. But we make a definite effort to catch something and *this is the corresponding element in our emotions.* When a fisherman pulls something he does not want from the water, he throws back the unwanted denizen of the ocean and no longer worries about it, transferring his *attention* to other things, which he prefers. In both cases he *acts*! And this means will-power in action.

Our friends who caught unwanted emotions, apparently act differently. They do not reject the approaching vibrations of the emotions which they dislike, as they say, but grant them their full attention, allowing them to occupy their whole consciousness, at the time. If so, are they not the *acting* element themselves, and do they not exercise their will-power, albeit unconsciously? If I put my finger into the fire intentionally or by accident, the result will be the same : a certain burning of the finger, with pain and other consequences.

Will-power has not merely a clear and fully conscious character. Often reality may be the opposite. However, the essence remains the same, and that is what I wanted to deduce from the simple examples just given.

A *conscious* man, that is, one who does not act impulsively, but who weighs everything he accepts and rejects, is the best endowed to make real experiments in the astral matter. Possessing the essential ability, which is that of *concentration* or *one-pointedness* in his consciousness, such a man would, by his own will, create different emotions, destroying them as he wishes, and thereby proving to himself what was said in the simile of the fisherman and his catch.

When such a man becomes an occultist—meaning one who practises occult theories on himself—he will then know infinitely more about the astral plane. In my former books I supplied plenty of details regarding the activities accessible to man in the astral plane, so there is no reason to repeat them again. Therefore, I will pass directly to the culminating moment of man's astral activities—his *exteriorization*, a deliberate and conscious leaving of the physical body and subsequent functioning in the astral vehicle, often called the 'astrosome' among occultists. This word, which is of Greek origin, usually denotes what we know as the 'astral body'. This experiment, which is also a considerable achievement for every occultist, is a proof of the astral world and life theory, just as a nuclear explosion is a proof and justification of the atomic theory.

But all inner processes in our consciousness are principally *subjective* ones, and cannot be tested by others, at least, not by those who have not had similar experiences, in other words, who do not know as much as we do.

This must be firmly recognized and realized, if we are to pass on successfully to further discussion of the subject.

The exteriorization of the astrosome simply means that man is able to forget the lower, that is, physical surroundings, or worlds, and to function consciously in the next higher one—the astral plane. On the present degree of evolution we are, in general, not supposed to transfer ourselves into the astral, for it has its own population, which evolves on that plane, just as we do on the physical. From this we can see that our true aim, the attainment of Samadhi, is not identical with astral travelling. Moreover, the best exponents of spiritual wisdom (very advanced Christian Saints, Eastern Yogis and especially the Perfect Men—Jivanmuktas or Great Rishis) do not advise us even to try these doubtful paths of peering into worlds where we are not supposed to live while still in the physical body (see *Concentration*, Parts II and IV). Such activities do not help us to achieve Samadhi, but rather distract our attention and thereby make our path unnecessarily longer.

Another world beyond the astral and physical ones is that of mental matter, interpenetrating both of the others because of its much lower density. When we think, we are functioning on this plane, while still being alive and active in our physical bodies. But we do not see the proper surroundings of the mental world, because we cannot divide our attention equally on more than one plane. This, of course, applies to the average man. Those who have tried successfully to obtain the consciousness of such a subtle world as is the mental one, may also be successful and able to perform exteriorization, not only into the *astral*, but equally well into the *mental*. This is much more difficult, and is impossible for ethically unripe people. This means that a black magician can work well and live consciously (while still in the physical body) in the *astral*, but he *cannot* exteriorize himself into the *mental*. Why? Simply because he does not possess the needed subtlety of thinking, for his aims and ideas are too gross and clumsy in comparison with the fine vibrations of the mental plane.

Great philosophers and very advanced occultists are able to spend considerably more time on the mental plane than on the physical. This calls for a special ability and the delight to think in very abstract currents of mind, otherwise, to live in the very rarefied atmosphere of the upper regions of thought and ideas. Traditionally, men like Plato are supposed to dwell in that heaven of fine thinkers for many thousands of earthly years.

And again, do you think that these heights are identical with Samadhi? Surely *not*! Listen to what the Great Rishi Ramana says, attempting to express the inexpressible truth of Samadhi: 'There is only the feeling *I am* but no thoughts.' Because of the sublime simplicity of this axiom you can attempt to gain some idea about the state of the Superconsciousness when you act as follows: expel all thoughts and remain with your own ultimate core of being—your *Self*!

That is the way which is used by many Eastern disciples of true spiritual Masters. Actually, it is not at all so simple in practice, for there are many prerequisites which must be reached before Samadhi can be attained. The foremost is the ability of full domination of one's mind, for a definite length of time, not measured in minutes, but in hours.

Now, are the theories about the three worlds in which humans function as separate entities, necessary for reaching the heights of Samadhi? Strictly speaking, no! Because it has been reached by men who had never even heard about the higher worlds. In fact, the ideal conditions for an earnest student are: to pass to the experience of the *Real* (which is just Samadhi) without stopping at the intermediate stages of the astral and mental planes.

This attitude is rather an Eastern one, but the writer prefers it to the Western, which recommends the gradual conscious passing through of all the planes, until the aim is reached.

Western masters (especially those of the classical and most developed branch of occultism, which is Hermetism) are usually of the opinion that an overwhelming number of men cannot pass into the *fourth* state without being acquainted with the intermediate ones.

But we can also reason in another way: if our aim, which will lead us to Samadhi, is the recognition of the illusion of Maya, which has to be overcome in this physical world, then for which purpose would we investigate other worlds, no matter how subtle they might be? Maya is always Maya, so the earlier one rejects it, the better for oneself.

On this note we will finish our present chapter about the higher worlds beyond the physical one.

Chapter IV

Different Forms Enveloping the Seat of Consciousness in Man

Verse 65: 'Without dissolving the world of objects, without knowing spiritual truth, where is eternal liberation from mere external words having no result beyond their mere utterance?'

PRACTICALLY, what does the term 'consciousness' mean to us? Theoretical somersaults will not cast much light on this problem. Leaving all learned definitions aside for the moment, we will seek the nearest expression for that consciousness. Nevertheless, we must be careful, and not confuse it with another similar (but utterly different in meaning) term—*awareness,* and to set up a practical line of separation between both of them.

(1) *Awareness* presupposes that we are aware of something, that is, that we know and feel its presence. I can be aware of the presence of a man in my room, even if it is completely dark, or if I have my eyes deliberately closed. This means that I know something apart from myself. You may add, that there is a visible *binary* in the awareness: I and Non-I, and this would be quite correct. Hermetic philosophy occupies itself with very meticulous studies of the laws directing *binaries,* ternaries and quarternaries, as a basis for important metaphysical and occult operations. Here there is no place to delve deeper into them, but I have spoken more about this theme in another of my works *The Tarot, a Contemporary Course of the Quintessence of Hermetic Occultism.*

(2) *Consciousness* builds another pole of the binary, one element of which was awareness. Here one is less (or almost not) dependent upon the *Non-I.* Consciousness belongs to our innermost *core,* without which we are—*nothing*! No one would agree to accept nothingness as a substitute for his consciousness, that is for *himself.* Therefore, rejecting all mental conceptions for a time, we can say: *consciousness is the clearest and most unique term,* which I can identify as myself, for it always remains with me, in all the normal conditions of my life. I can experience this or that, be aware or not aware of

some object, thought or feeling, but I cannot—without being converted into 'nothing'—lose my consciousness. Immediately someone will object : 'Well, but when I am under anaesthetics, or when I am in deep sleep, I cannot find any consciousness of myself, and then I am without any consciousness at all.'

This comment is only apparently true. Not all of us are devoid of self-consciousness in the aforementioned states, although such people are still in the minority among average men. There are too many confirmed reports by people, who, although under full anaesthetics or merged in deep sleep without dreams, did not lose their consciousness or cease to exist completely in these particular conditions.

I also know of this from my own experience, as well as from that of many others, about which they have told me. The development of a high degree of concentration substantially contributes to separation of the conditioned and unconditioned elements in man. Moreover, *Samadhi*—the very subject of the present study, is the foremost example of *existence*, that is, of being self-conscious, beyond all bodily and mental conditions.

All of this has been said in order to elucidate the term 'seat of Consciousness', which is used in the title of this chapter.

But, are we—as we feel ourselves every day—just that seemingly abstract consciousness, which can be best formulated as that magic axiom—*I am*? Certainly not, at least, not now, at our present level of evolution. We are compelled to accept and to confess to this fact, if we are to be sincere, and if we have not yet attained the realization of the *Self* in us. And this, simply because, if we possessed this high degree of inner development, we would not read this book, just as a professor would not study a primer.

This means that there are things like veils which envelop the pure consciousness in man. Ask the first man you meet, who he is? The answer will primarily contain his name. What is hidden under this label of personality, which is our name? It is worth analysing more attentively.

(1) The first and chief envelope of our deepest seat of consciousness is, of course, our physical body, with all its individual properties and qualities such as our sex. We invariably feel ourselves to be men or women, but evidently we cannot ascribe to our consciousness—which we find to be beyond this veil—any awareness of being either male or female. Here I am excluding dreams because they are fairly exact reflections of our waking life, at least, for the greatest majority of people. The next label is our age (physical). It is only natural, that in identifying ourselves with the body, we accept its age as an integral part of us.

From these come the whole complex of other details to form the personality-ego, attached by our erratic thinking to the individual being in us. Take our education. If our brain has been trained say in mathematics, foreign languages, or any other subject, we are usually convinced that all of them are *components* of our person, like our outer appearance, and so on. Social and family position also apparently belong to the same human ego. The overwhelming majority believes in it, often subconsciously, as only a few are able and willing to put before themselves even *once* in their lives, the controversial question : who am I? This short formula has terrific power. It is impossible to give all its applications here, simply because, if we think deeper about this theme, we find that there is no end to the mental processes which arise if we use this inquiry even just with our mind. Nevertheless, we will speak about it several times in the course of this book, because the very answer to it lies in the absence of words and thoughts which is just *Samadhi* (also called the Egoless State) as was truly said by the Great Rishi Ramana.

(2) The *second* envelope (or veil) which we wear, apart from the physical one, is our emotional life and its properties. We have to be careful and not confuse them with mind and its functions, even if both might be closely connected and welded together in everyday life, as often happens in practice.

Despite this fact, both are quite distinctly different powers and kinds of matter, and we can never reach any logical and positive conclusion without being trained in discrimination between feelings and thoughts (or astral and mental, as occultists say). Now I will give a series of examples which may help us to draw conclusions more easily.

Imagine that one morning you are looking at a charming garden, with green lawns, flowers and spring freshness surrounding its beds and paths. A peculiarly pleasant feeling may arise in us, which has still not been transferred into thoughts, and later words and deeds. Only that *spring feeling*, a pure feeling alone. And this will be that something which explains the purely emotional realm and reactions in our consciousness. Try this experience for yourself, modifying it according to your own ideas, and adding as many examples as you think may be necessary, in order to become somewhat acquainted with the idea of the *astral* in and apart from you. Pure astral currents are usually pleasant and refreshing. Often they are connected with some special environments, conditions and places. And you can easily check this.

The countryside, beautiful vistas, abundant and lovely flowers, and so on, all may be taken into consideration and the astral currents arising in their proximity can be registered and analysed. Now take another source of the astral currents in you. Read a book (travel, poetry, and so on, but *not* a scientific one) finding descriptions which create emotional feelings in you. Understand and register them in your memory, then deliberately try to evoke them by an effort of your will. There is no need to label these astral currents, because any mixing of them with mental elements means a spoiling of the purely astral impressions.

As you have no doubt gathered by now, it is essential that you learn to discriminate about the veils which envelop your core of consciousness as exactly as possible. Probably, you have already guessed the purpose of these simple exercises: *to give you certain practical knowledge of the title of this chapter.* An understanding of the elementary processes in man's consciousness is essential when we seek an approach to the higher consciousness, realized in *Samadhi.*

This is an axiom, which should be remembered throughout the study of the following chapters of this book.

In order to finish with the astral forms of the envelopes veiling the pure consciousness in us, deliberately and artificially try to create different emotions like love and hatred, attraction and repulsion, rest and restlessness, satisfaction and desire, peace and turmoil, and so on. Start with the name of the feeling, then remember your past impressions related to the required creation as this may be helpful. At first, you will probably not immediately be able to perform all of this, and some effort will be necessary as regards the reliving of emotions as advised in the previous sentence. Advanced people can dispense with memory, and create the astral currents *ad libitum.*

The true aim is to create 'from nothing'. This also requires many former experiences of feelings, which should be well memorized in the subconscious counterpart of our astral body, so that projection comes without any previous deliberations.

I have given the basic feelings in pairs, the first element in each pair being a *positive* feeling, and the second its *negative* counterpart like love and hatred. Try to shorten the negative part as much as possible and do not think about it afterwards. But the exercises would be one-sided, thereby having lowered value, if I were to give only the so-called good feelings for study. In this case you might be helpless against negative currents, if you have no acquaintance with them and the method for their removal. This should be taken from *Concentration* (Part II) where it has been fully explained and all the necessary protective measures given.

The third form in which the pure consciousness clothes itself, is the world of thoughts, the realm of the mind, or the 'mental plane' according to occultists. To it belongs all that we *think* and consequently say, but without adding any emotional stress. Again, the astral and mental interpenetrate one another very much, and it is not possible for an untrained person to make the necessary discrimination between these two planes. Therefore we have to pass on to some elementary exercises.

Firstly, count slowly, pronouncing the numbers in your mind and at the same time imagining each one suddenly appearing before your eyes as a white figure on a black background. Start with 1 and continue for as far as your time and will-power allow you. It is easy if one has a little good will and desire for the cognition of some essential processes in one's own mind. Take simple numbers at first, projecting them on to the dark screen in your imagination. You can close your eyes if you feel it will be easier for you. And so begin: one (1), two (2), three (3), and so on for as long as you can. For the first exercise take from one to twenty and then later up to fifty. Do it slowly, without any haste and without thinking about anything except the numbers. When performing it you are acting purely in a subdivision of the mental plane (or world), and using the matter of only that plane. There are surely no feelings in such an exercise and that is just what is needed. Next time, think about another simple process, with which no emotions can possibly be connected. For example, repeat in your mind the process of dressing after you arise from bed in the morning; walk and concentrate on counting your steps for some three to five minutes; choose a suitable vantage point and from it count passing cars or trains.

The second series will be to repeat all of the aforementioned in your memory only, by the process of creative imagination.

Finally, as by now you have surely learned, to a certain extent, to distinguish thoughts from feelings, try to create purely mental processes in your mind, according to your choice. These can be some of your future activities, reviewed as if from the past.

The latter might be somewhat dangerous as one is subconsciously liable to add astral vibrations to mental ones, that is, join one's emotions to one's thoughts, which is not permitted for our present purpose. If you have realized the aim of this chapter well, you will acquire the ability of practical separation from the discrimination about all the three worlds in which you actually live, until you abandon all of them for Samadhi.

Then you will *know* which form-veils throw shadows on your true and pure consciousness, and you will also know what stand as obstacles on your way to Samadhi. In other words, what you have to reject before you can reach this lofty state.

Although, when it is attained, Samadhi transcends all human knowledge, one of the approaches to it can be scientific and the student should know about it. Of course, in itself, it is not sufficient, for there are other conditions which must be realized, and other approaches which should also be tried. The following chapters will describe these.

To conclude, we may say that the seat of the physical consciousness (waking state, called *Jagrat* by the Hindus) in an average man is his brain. This has been defined in my previous books as well as in the present as *Brain-consciousness*. Emotions and feelings find their fulcrum in the corresponding astral counterpart (or body), while the mind's functions are generated in the mental body, from which they pass to the brain and into the waking state. Details can be found in *Concentration*, for those who would like to investigate the problem more exactly. For the present study, belonging expressly to the 'fourth' state or Samadhi, the information given in brief here will suffice.

In Hindu sacred Scriptures, there are many Upanishads, Gitas and treatises which doubtless can induce Samadhi. But when and in whom? Certainly not in quite raw beginners who, because of unpreparedness, are not in a position to decipher the holy texts, which do not speak in 'open language', just the same as occult manuals, which always have a veil, thereby guarding the contents from profanation and misuse.

On this point I would recommend that the earnest student reads, with the utmost concentration, a few verses from *Ashtavakra Gita* translated into masterly English by the late Hari Prasad Shastri of London.

The original works of Sri Ramana Maharshi, such as his *Forty Verses* and *Truth Revealed*, are supreme, but not too easy to understand properly, if the student is not well acquainted with the philosophy of that contemporary Sage.

Chapter V

Modern Psychology and Its Methods

Verse 67: 'Hidden treasure does not come out at (utterance of) the simple word "out", but there must be trustworthy information, digging and removal of stones; similarly the pure truth, itself transcending the operation of *maya* (*maya* here meaning the force of evolution) is not obtained without the instruction of the knowers of the supreme, together with reflection, meditation, and so forth, and not by illogical inferences.'

OFFICIAL psychology is of no use in the study of Samadhi. There are many reasons for this. The *first* is that psychologists occupy themselves with the analysis of average men, who are simply ignorant of any transcendental experiences, and who have not studied the means which may lead to the Superconsciousness. If there are some unusual manifestations, like temporary siddhis (occult or psychic powers) in the form of visions, precognition, clairvoyance and mediumism, then all of them are sporadic and unpredictable phenomena and cannot be produced on request.

Their authenticity and cause cannot be scientifically investigated because of their highly subjective, rare and personal character, which therefore cannot be duly classified and explained.

The *second* is that psychology operates mainly on the emotional and partly in the mental realms in man, that is, on the astral and mental manifestations which find a visible and audible form for any investigator, endowed with only the 'normal' means of cognition and operation. How can this be of any use in a case, where the aim transcends both these planes, as Samadhi is far above and beyond all feelings and thoughts?

One who has not experienced the *Superconsciousness* for himself cannot speak about it with any authority, or even give explanations about a subject utterly unknown to him.

The *third* is because we normally operate in our three planes of existence with only the means supplied by the same planes. Taking into consideration the highest abilities of the average man, which are his mental powers, we see that they have certain, but limited methods of cognition, like *a priori* and *a posteriori* judgements, logical conclusions, and former experiences, all of which, in every case, require further development of our knowledge. They are all of a purely relative character connected with this and not another form of existence, that is, the human one.

A modern Indian philosopher Sri Aurobindo Ghose (who died in 1950) said rightly in one of his aphorisms:

'When we have passed beyond humanity, then we shall be the Man. . . .'

A psychologist operates with his brain on persons endowed with similar instruments, which belong to the world of physical matter. This is only natural in physical conditions. But in the Superconsciousness we are further from the mind's limited means and its objects of cognition, than any galaxy is from our physical mother—earth.

When a psychologist tries to classify his experiences in order to deduce some laws from them, which later can be applied to all his patients, he collects them principally from books containing the results of experiments by other specialists, plus his own findings, necessarily limited to the circle of living brains which he investigates. He himself does not possess and cannot offer us any *direct knowledge* of these things.

And all knowledge which still operates with things is *incompatible* with the state of Samadhi, just as a cube cannot be compressed into a square, because of the difference in dimensions between both the geometrical elements.

Eternal Consciousness is a continuous one, no matter which forms sometimes surround the manifestation. Psychology deals only with *manifestations*, being created by similar temporary ones which we call—when still alive—*human beings*: just like soap-bubbles, which form only to burst and cease to reflect colours on their fragile surfaces.

But Samadhi, as we will see in the following chapters, is a result of transcending all movements in the brain, as well as in the astral and mental planes of man. Therefore, in wishing to get closer to Samadhi, we must seek for more adequate training and methods than modern psychology and official 'science' can offer for the purpose. So our ways and aims are very different, and I have expounded them for beginners in another of my books—*Concentration*.

Chapter VI

The Two Ways Before Us

Verse 80: 'He who is free from the great bondage of desires, so difficult to avoid, is alone capable of liberation; not another, even though versed in the six systems of philosophy.'

ONLY male beings, exceptionally advanced in evolution, come into this world endowed with the Superconsciousness, or—Samadhi. Even they do not experience it immediately after their physical birth, but usually after adolescence, as they mature into early manhood. History knows nothing about any women possessing Samadhi in their youth.

So it was with Christ and Maharshi. But the reader, as well as the writer, is quite naturally concerned most of all with his own case, that is, his own incarnation at the present time, and this is only right. Anyway, you and I were not born with the Superconsciousness as our inherited property. This means that if one wants to acquire it, one has to make definite efforts in that direction.

It would be impossible if we do not know many things about the object of our strivings.

In this chapter, called The Two Ways Before Us, we will become acquainted with *positive qualities* and conditions, which give us chances of success, as well as with *negative ones*, which make attainment impossible at the time. There are three basic types of men, which we can distinguish.

The *first* and the *third* types have only one way, but the *second* stands before two paths and until he reaches the aim, is compelled to tread both of them. What are these two ways?

A. Look around yourself. What are the human masses striving for in this world? Do they know anything about Samadhi and do they seek after it? Certainly not! It is impossible to describe in full detail all the desires obsessing humanity today. But it can be done in broad outline. If there are exceptions (and they are unavoidable), they will not affect the general rules, which we will now establish.

When childhood comes to an end, everyone finds that life begins to require certain solutions to many problems connected with the physical existence. We can enumerate them in brief. If one is not rich from birth, one must look for some means of existence and support. Here also belong our educational efforts, sometimes coloured by the 'thirst for knowledge', which puts bread-winning interests in second place. In our younger years, sexual life often plays an important role. Then comes the desire to establish some firm material basis, to obtain honours, highly placed connections, and so on. When, together with advancing age, ailments develop, combating them may occupy the last years of a man's life. It is true that a few also have some idealistic tendencies, usually vague, and always connected with the species called 'Homo sapiens'.

All of this has a common line: *egoism*, or actions—directly or indirectly—touching on the *ego-individuality* of the doer. Then man is, or is not, satisfied with his personal achievements, is happy or is miserable, but everything in him invariably revolves round the visible, tangible, material world.

On this level of development, people have only *one* way—a material existence from birth to death. The latter being considered as the greatest, but inevitable evil. This way does not allow a man any transcendental search for another aspect of life, say, a conscious striving to develop one's consciousness beyond the narrow limitations of the ego-life in matter. Therefore, the question of Samadhi cannot be taken into consideration with this category of men. This is because they are uniform in their materialism, and do not feel any duality as yet.

In them, the philosophic conceptions of *unity* in aims takes the lowest form, unlike the third category of highly evolved men, those fully spiritualized ones, who are rare sources of light in the darkness of spiritual night. These people have also only *one* way, but it is diametrically opposed to the way of life of the first category, which has just been described. We will speak about this different kind of *unity* after we have analysed the next, the *second class*, as follows.

B. When man becomes dissatisfied with the line of existence like that of category A, important questions begin to arise in his mind. In general these have the following pattern: Where is the beginning of life? What is the aim of life? What comes after death? Which reasons are there for the existence of the human species on this planet? What relations occur between the Microcosm (man) and the Macrocosm (universe) and many other similar questions which are difficult to enumerate.

All of them have a common point: these problems transcend the *narrow ego-life*. Some people apparently find answers in their religions, and then they do not seek independently, relying on the dogmas and explanations given by their churches. We will leave this group apart, as they are not active in the spiritual search, believing that they have already found the true way. It is exclusively their own business.

But there are those who are not satisfied with any ready-made solutions, and begin to search for themselves, trying to experience what they have read about the higher states of consciousness, that lie beyond the physical and other planes. Sometimes such seekers encounter the idea of Superconsciousness—Samadhi, and follow it. So arises the *second* type of man, the seeker after spiritual truth, spiritual life, despite the fact that he is still dwelling—at least partially—in dense matter through the intermediary of his body. If this is the case with you, then you are already separated from the first ('A') group, which has only one purpose, that is material life. It is all too evident that we cannot look for seekers of Samadhi in the first group.

The seekers come from the second group 'B', and it is with them that we will now be occupied, in this part of the present chapter.

Now a seeker (as we will term a man of the second group) receives some inner enlightenment and then begins to realize that he cannot trust his mortal counterpart, which did not exist before his birth and will not exist after his death. He is now wise enough not to drug himself with the 'agnostic' idea of annihilation of his consciousness-self together with the physical body. Perhaps as yet, not having any direct experience of the immortal truth of existence (which comes much later) he already feels intuitively where his sure refuge lies. For, at this stage, his karma usually allows him to enter into contact with a suitable spiritual teaching, or even—in very rare cases—with a living Master himself, if such a being is on our planet in his physical body at that time.

But, usually, the original written, or spoken doctrine plus sometimes the co-operation of more advanced disciples of the same Guru is the lot of aspirants. This step often brings much enthusiasm and happiness intensified to the pitch where there are flashes of bliss. I think it is a very wise arrangement on the side of the *Guiding Power*, for the Path itself is a thorny one, because karma must be quickly discharged in order to set a man more free for the strenuous spiritual work ahead, unhindered by karmic repercussions and obstacles.

So, initial ecstasies give the first essential push ahead, which in many cases should suffice for the lifetime. Remembrance of that bliss brings solace to the disciple in hard times, allowing him to remain unbroken under the blows of fate.

This circumstance is well known to all who enter on the Path. I experienced it years before I faced the Master in his physical body, that is, received his permanent Darshan. This bliss usually came unexpectedly, and not when one would like to have it. *Spiritus flat ubi vult* remains a true axiom in the realm of spiritual search.

On some evenings when travelling long distances by bus in far-off South America, this inner wonder came of itself, bringing peace beyond all, bliss without measure. The normal consciousness was not at all dimmed, and there were no visions : this was the best proof of the reality of these first glimpses into the Superconsciousness, as taught by the Master Maharshi. It lasted about five to fifteen minutes, seldom more. It influenced not only the experiencer, but also the surroundings in a truly mystical way. In Chapter XLVII of *In Days of Great Peace* we read :

> 'It is interesting to note that this state has its own range of vibrations, extremely subtle and powerful. They influence our surroundings; we can easily observe their effect on people when we experience, however imperfectly, this state ourselves. When, being at the very threshold of the Samadhi sunrise [beginning] we talk to others, or when we just emerge from the Samadhi sunset [final phase], we can notice that people are behaving—probably unconsciously—somewhat differently, and addressing us in another tone than usual, although from without they can see nothing save our "normal" ordinary persons. But each one has his own Samadhi deep in his heart in a latent state, which one day will reveal itself. Thus this "dormant" germ of the Spirit responds to the vibrations of the spirit awakened.'

Such is the beginning. And now the title of this chapter comes to mind—The Two Ways Before Us. For, from this time forward, we will always live as if continuously at the cross-roads. Let us not be mistaken about the meaning of these words as used here. It means, that while knowing about the absolute superiority of the immaterial, spiritual consciousness in himself, the disciple will be constantly confronted with the karmic elements of his actual incarnation, apparently bringing disappointment, bitterness, sometimes even driving a man close to despair. But in vain ! The true Path cannot be lost. It can be dimmed, if we are too unwise, and allow the mirage of the visible and sensible world to gain the upper hand. But finally, the erring son will return to his spiritual father, as beautifully described by Christ, and explained by the Maharshi : 'Who once enters on the Path cannot lose it, just as the prey which falls into the tiger's jaws will never be allowed to escape.'

I would like to remind all those who are struggling at the cross-roads of Attainment about this, and so let them regain their peace when they hear the words of the Masters.

At this time, the most unusual circumstances will face a man. His environment may become hostile to him because of his new attitude, which will cause him to neglect certain aspects of worldly life; friends may betray him and men may hold him in contempt without any apparent reason. But know O disciple! The Prince of this world does not forgive those who try to escape from his power. One must face him, and win or fall away for a period of time known as a 'spiritual eclipse'. Those who fall away sometimes become erring souls for many incarnations. And yet they return, with bleeding feet and hearts, and always they come back to the point from which they deserted. We will not delve into this theme any more, closing the problem with the statement that, *the price of erring is high.*

However, the bulk of temptations do not come from active interference on the part of the Enemy, but from everyday life, when we are confronted with apparently petty problems which, nevertheless, must be solved according to the new consciousness dawning in us.

I am deliberately refraining from speaking here about Samadhi, leaving it to later chapters in Parts III and IV of this book, when the student should be better equipped to face the ultimate problem of life.

But a few examples can be given:

(a) *Should we retaliate against those who harm us?*
At this stage we are, as has been said before, at the cross-roads, on a double way. One belongs to the world, another to the Spirit. So I will also give you the apparent solution in dual form.
(1) Never retaliate, but rather avoid the offenders.
(2) Turn the other cheek to the offenders as taught Christ.
Which of these two solutions would be yours? No one can say, apart from yourself. This also applies to all the following examples.

(b) *What should be done if your surroundings or even family set up active resistance, or obstacles, to your new way of life?*
(1) The Path should be kept a secret one from all except the Master and his other disciples. It is chiefly an inner Path. It is easier to prevent difficulties than to fight them later.
(2) 'Render therefore to Caesar the things that are Caesar's; and to God, the things that are God's.'

(c) *What should be done when sensual temptations befall you and you feel humiliation and are afraid of succumbing to them?*

39

(1) Read a spiritual work when you are attacked by impure forces. Meditate about lofty matters which inspire you. Use direct means of defence (see *Concentration*, Parts II and IV).
(2) Remember 'who you are' (read Chapters XXXIV and XLVIII of *In Days of Great Peace*).

*   *   *   *

The next kinds of obstacles come from the side of your own mind. Theoretically, the disciple already knows that he and his mind are two different things. But to know it practically means not less than to reach full domination of the thinking process, which happens only at the end of the Path, just before Attainment of Mastership. Therefore, the double-tracked way preceding it, is filled with fights for supremacy over the mind. The latter uses innumerable tricks in order to disrupt the attention of those who want to become its (mind's) masters.

Questions arise in us, which, when analysed properly, appear futile, unnecessary and often insoluble. The most common type is concerned with the endless *whys*. Why this thing is such and not another? Why obstacles bar our way? Why we cannot come at once to the end of the Path?

You can find further development of these *whys* for yourself. But the wise person summarily rejects all of them, concentrating his attention on the essential work of self-development, because he knows that all questions will disappear for ever when he reaches the *wisdom*, instead of seeking after relative knowledge.

The *duality* surrounding this *second* type of man, who is *en route* to the *third* and final group, where all the lessons have been learned, is undoubtedly tragic. All occultists know about it, and many have described it in their outstanding works. Among these I would like to mention only the famous *Zanoni* by Bulwer Lytton.

The best means for understanding this problem, which is a binary, is to look attentively at our own consciences. In classical occult philosophic literature I could not find anything as beautiful and full of the wisdom of the human psyche as Plotinus' *Enneades*. In the beginning the sage gives general advice, which is very suitable for every aspirant and disciple:

'Enter into thyself and look; and if thou are not yet beautiful, do as does the sculptor with his statue: he smooths this line, he planes another, giving a nobler expression, until the whole becomes the resplendent picture of perfect beauty. And thou shouldst do the same.'

C. It now remains to discuss the *third* type of man, that is, he who has finished with all the toil and experiences of the *second* group; who has learned everything up to the degree of Wisdom, which transcends all relative knowledge, and realizes, as a necessary consequence, that there is nothing more for him to learn. For perfection does not need any additions or changes. He has reached the perennial Samadhi, being the state of spiritual consciousness which has become permanent, an unchangeable privilege of the Perfect Being or Master, as we may call him. The aim and possibility for us, who still belong to the *second* type, is the same Samadhi; but in our present state of discipleship, we can hope only for *temporary* flights into the land of the Real, Eternal and Bliss. Even this is already a very big step ahead, as one who has experienced *Kevala Nirvikalpa Samadhi* (that is, temporary formless Superconsciousness) even once, has been changed for ever. This is because it is impossible to erase the memory of Samadhi. We can experience it once in our lives, or even every day, and this will not change the rule. Samadhi (of the Kevala type) can be lived only when all the functions of the body are reduced to the barest possible minimum, which means their temporary suspension. The body becomes immobile, sometimes stiff; breathing has very long periods between inhaling and exhaling, and, for a while, may even stop altogether. But the permanent type (Sahaja Samadhi), being the unique privilege of perfect Masters, discards all limitations of the body and is experienced at all times, no matter whether the body is awake or asleep, alive or dead. As you and I do not belong to the very small number of Perfect Ones, we cannot have the experience and exact knowledge of the Sahaja. It is still a mystery for us, how one can live for ever in that sublime state and at the same time be free of all the limitations imposed on us, when we perform our highest flights into the Kevala. Therefore it is useless to guess about it. Let us be satisfied with the certain hope, that the Great Day will come for us, when no shadow will remain and when we will be for ever in the Light, becoming that Light ourselves. There is no other way.

All this does not apply to the undeveloped *unity* in aims and life, belonging to the primitive type A, for whom everything has still to be attained, for this last type is beyond the world of binaries of the second group (B), reaching the *absolute unity* of the All-Wisdom. Its oneness is attained for ever. All lower states are transcended and forgotten. They become obsolete. These are only words, of course, but what immensity of achievement lies hidden in them. All the Highest, about which we can only guess and hope, has become a glorious reality. There is no longer the body to be an obstacle, for Consciousness-Self has reached the primordial purity and perfection. We say that we have one consciousness or another. But here it is the Consciousness which possesses everything, being itself unattached to anything. It is simply the *One* without a *second*.

Sir Edwin Arnold expressed this very well when, in his *The Light of Asia*, he speaks of the dew-drop falling from the lotus leaf into the radiant ocean of the Whole ('Om mani padme hum, the sunrise comes ! The dewdrop slips into the shining sea !'). But this happens only when the 'drops' (that is, you and I) become so pure, that their dissolution in the Ocean becomes possible without the spoiling of its eternally crystalline purity. These, of course, are only similies, because Realization of Attainment transcends all speech and thought, object and subject, time and space. That is the true *oneness* in Samadhi.

*   *   *   *

As we can see, only a man of the *second* type (B) can choose his way. The *first* type (A) is unripe, while the *third* (C) is beyond all. An undeveloped person from the first group does not know, and does not want to know, anything which transcends his narrow egoistic aims and life, dedicated as these are to material business and pleasures, when he can get them. So he does not have any choice simply because he does not choose. That is why true occultists never try to 'convert' anyone to their own convictions, knowledge and theories which they consider to be just. It would be as useless as trying to explain the beauty of a picture to a blind person. However, karma itself looks after this and usually does not put this group into contact with the superior types. But it is a different case with the *second* group. These men can encounter books, lectures and finally, other men concerned with the advancement of life in themselves. If you find spiritual literature which absorbs you, or meet a *man on the Path*, it is a sure sign that, in you, there are already some germs of higher life, which await development. In other words, you are invited to pass into the *second* group (B), that of the 'seekers'.

In this instance I am alluding to a genuine search and not a superficial, fleeting interest in certain phenomena of occult origin, hypnotic tricks, fortune-telling, ghost stories, and so on.

A serious search is always based on seeking a solution to the mystery *belonging to your own being*, which so far, is like the smile of the Sphinx for you. This is because no earnest and successful search can be initiated and conducted without the basic element of *Self-knowledge*. In modern occult literature there are plenty of references to it. Spiritual Masters also place much value on that search :

> 'For what doth it profit a man, if he gain the whole world, and suffer the loss of his own soul? Or what exchange shall a man give for his soul?' (St Matthew, 16, 26.)

It is for you to define to which type of human being you belong. And if it happens to be the *second* group, do not forget about the right starting point of all knowledge : *the search for yourself!*

But day after day is passing, and our way to the end of wandering in this visible world becomes shorter and shorter. This means that the final account for the lessons of life comes closer with every day, until there will be the last one. Then we will be confronted with the accomplished facts, which cannot be changed any more, and the balance must be struck, which will be the last act of the incarnation's drama.

For us, will it be a victorious march, with head held high, into the other manifestation of life, in full acquired knowledge and Light, or just erring in darkness and fear, being only the natural continuation of a frustrated past?

Chapter VII

What Brings the Ecstasy?

Verse 84: 'If the desire for liberation exists in thee, sensuous objects must be left at a great distance as if they were poison, thou must constantly and fervently seek contentment as if it were ambrosia, also kindness, forgiveness, sincerity, tranquillity and self-control.'

WHEN writing on a subject which is so difficult for most readers, such as is Samadhi, we have to elucidate all the terms which are often confused with it. One of the most misleading is that of ecstasy. Samadhi is often called 'ecstasy' and hence visionary ecstasies are mistakenly understood to be Samadhi.

The truth is that both terms, and consequently the corresponding states of consciousness, are two different and incommensurable things. Throughout this work we will find sufficient explanations and material about Samadhi, therefore this chapter will be dedicated to the great grand-daughter of Samadhi, which is ecstasy.

The actual meaning of it is 'rapture', which is exact and is used in psychological terminology, as well as for our purpose here. When a man finds himself in ecstasy, he feels that he is in a spiritual rapture, that is, beyond his normal senses and perceptions, which then become for him as an unreal dream of the past.

It is the accepted thing, to connect ecstasy with blissful experiences, with intense feelings of happiness. In general this is true. But ecstasy usually has some definite (often material) causes. We know about the rapture of love, of self-surrender, of artistic elation, and so on. The experience seems to depend upon a particular property in man, that is, when the emotional side of him is predominant. We cannot easily imagine any kind of ecstasy overwhelming a cold, dry and unimaginative person, whose inner world is rather dull and unimpressive, and we will be right.

At this point we can consider the so-called spiritual ecstasy, about which we may learn more from the lives of some of the saints. And then we will find that not all of these outstanding men experienced any visible rapture when merged in prayers or contemplation.

If everyone in the environment of, say, St Francis of Assisi, or St Theresa, or St John the Apostle, and so on, was able to perceive in them their ecstatic states, the same thing could hardly be said about other types of saints, like St Jean de Vianney, St Seraphim of Sarov and the Maharshi. When the latter answered questions about the exact meaning of ecstasy, he pointed out: 'When the mind is transcended and the consciousness therefore merges into Samadhi, there cannot be any ecstasy at all, for the very element which can experience it (that is, the mind) in Samadhi is *absent*. But, when Samadhi comes to its end and the mind emerges again, it often happens that the ecstasy appears. This is because the mind is then enlightened by the reflection of the unimaginable spiritual bliss of true Superconsciousness, devoid of all forms and limitations.' In Hindu terminology it is called Kevala Nirvikalpa Samadhi, which is a very exact and full definition. Such ecstasies are often connected with tears of bliss, laughter, tremors of the body, rapturous singing, and so on.

Now we may better understand the differences and relationships of both: Samadhi and ecstasy. The *first* is essential and all-important for those who are able to reach it. The *second* is a *reflection and manifestation* of the transcendental, unchanging and supreme state in one's mind and emotions, in other words, in the astral and mental planes. I am referring here to the higher form of ecstasy, and not any lower ones, which sometimes occur as a result of happy circumstances of all kinds in one's personal life. Some have the emotional upheaval because of happy love affairs, a big monetary win (in a lottery, and so on), and similar conditions. If we analyse our own little inner ecstasies well we will almost invariably find their origin in sources similar to those just mentioned. To summarize, we may state that now we know from where ecstasy comes, and how to find its origin.

But there are still some other kinds which have a purely *mental* source. When a philosopher or scientist makes a very important discovery or invention, he too may get an ecstatic uplifting of *his mind*. Recall only those few known to us from history: Archimedes, who, when he found the solution to the problem of how to discover the specific weight of physical bodies, left his bath and in somewhat incomplete attire, ran down the street crying 'Eureka!', for he was then able to determine the true amounts of silver and gold in the king's crown.

Isaac Newton on discovering the basic physical law of gravity was also overwhelmed with joy, for at last he was able to formulate that law scientifically by observing an object falling to earth from a certain height. We are not sure if it really was an apple falling from a tree.

If we would like to summarize what has been said about *Samadhi* and *ecstasy*, a comparison such as 'light and reflection' would not be far from the truth, which otherwise is inexpressible in words. Important developments will come from this definition.

(a) We should always seek for the *source* or *reality* in our higher experiences, and not only for the side-effects.

(b) The primary source is Superconsciousness—Samadhi. It alone counts and is important.

(c) All the innumerable ecstasies are—in the best of cases—only derivatives of (b) and, apart from the pleasure which they may bring, cannot be considered as true factors of inner enlightenment.

(d) As all visions are only different forms of mental activity, with which we are so far not much acquainted, they cannot help us in our search for the eternal elements attainable in Samadhi, but rather they are distractions. They hinder concentration which is the basis for Superconsciousness, the latter requiring full domination—even if for a limited time—and elimination of the mind's vibratory activities in us.

All this is true even despite the fact that some form of visions may appear to be 'prophetic', that is, they may have in them a reflection of clichés from past, present or future happenings. The Western occultism known as 'Hermetism' has elaborated the field of visions well, and I spoke about them extensively in another of my books *The Tarot, a Contemporary Course of the Quintessence of Hermetic Occultism.*

The symbolic visions of St John in his 'Revelations', and those of Nostradamus are well known and striking by their accuracy, in spite of the somewhat cumbersome language of the latter (which is a mixture of old French and Latin), and the form in which they were given to posterity.

We may, of course, doubt in the practical wisdom of all prophecies, because they excite our curiosity rather than lead us to more careful and well-calculated activity. As an example, the fact can be cited, that Napoleon I and Hitler both knew the Nostradamus texts and could not possibly but recognize themselves in them. Nevertheless, they acted exactly as predicted, and therefore could not escape their fates, as mentioned in the prophecies. It is an interesting thought about which all amateurs of prophesying and fortune-telling should think deeply. Is there any reason to seek after these divinatory illusions, which cannot really influence the life and karma of humanity?

PART II

The Threshold and the First Steps

Chapter VIII

Justice in Actions and Intentions

Verse 420: 'The result of dispassion is right perception; of right perception abstention from the pleasures of sense and ceremonial acts. The peace that comes from the realization of the true is the fruit of abstention from ceremonial acts, from the pleasures of sense.'

ON reaching the end of the first part of this work, we finished with the definitions of terms, methods, phenomena and conditions which we may encounter on our way to Samadhi.

Now the inner preparation lies before us. Is it necessary? Yes, in every case, unless you belong to those few who come to this earth already enlightened in Wisdom, having achieved the final Light in their glorious past. This refers to the true spiritual Masters, one of whom I was privileged to see with my mortal eyes, a fact which has changed my whole life as well as that of a few others, who have preferred not to share the inner treasures they received from the Master with this cruel world; not to write, but to remain silent for ever. In this way they can avoid conflict with the world, which usually attacks the forerunners of human evolution by trying to silence their speech.

But: 'In my Father's house there are many mansions . . .' and different ways lead to them.

However, ways exist to be trodden upon, and this means *effort and movement.* And so it is with those who want to reach the aim before others, and who need to know about the first steps to be made in the direction of Samadhi. In *Concentration* can be found methods for development of the inner powers, enabling us to enter on the Path. These consist of different forms of concentration, which is the paramount one of all the inner forces in us.

As has already been said in the first chapter of this book, the earnest student, who himself actually endeavours to reach Samadhi (Superconsciousness) is supposed to perform Part III of *Concentration* satisfactorily. This is because Samadhi is the *'feeling I-I,* but no thoughts' as was taught by the contemporary master of it—Sri

Ramana Maharshi. This means that thoughts must be deliberately excluded from the mind before the desired state of consciousness can be reached. It is a condition. But how could one, not possessing the ability of concentration be successful in an attempt to cleanse the mind of thoughts? You see, it is a magic circle, which always brings us to the same fulcrum that has to be attained. There are other qualities in us which must be developed practically before we step over the holy threshold, which leads to the silent temple of Samadhi.

In the last chapter of *Concentration* I gave, as a theme for meditation, the seventeen 'Nirvana-Verses', without any further development, because they belong to the present work, and not to the former, which is only a preparation for this book.

Samadhi makes high demands upon the aspirant. This means that vices must be eradicated and basic virtues acquired. *Let us make no mistake*, these are *conditions*. If one still has plenty of negative qualities and few virtues (positive qualities), it is only proof that one's subtle bodies are crude, and their vibrations slow and clumsy. How can they harmonize with the absolute purity of the Superconsciousness? You cannot achieve Samadhi just because someone has shown you certain technicalities, used by advanced adepts, but which may not entirely suit you. Remember that, in Samadhi, you are transcending the humanity in yourself, reaching the state which perhaps others will need eons to obtain. Then, instead of as before, being limited and conditioned, you become the Infinite and Absolute. How great this task is!

Can such heights be attained at all? They can, simply because their attainment means nothing more than rejection of all the veils, which shadow the eternal and always perfect Atman-Self-Spirit in you. These three terms are synonymous.

If it were otherwise, no attainment would be possible, because the *Trinity*, as mentioned in the last sentence, *cannot be created or annihilated*. Realize that they are *eternal things*, always present and everywhere, beyond space and time. This process will need deep meditation, before you enter into the right current with your consciousness, which will then reveal to you what I am trying to convey with words at this moment. But words cannot give you the realization of that truth, only your own inner effort. Perform it now, and then read further.

By extending this analysis, you will see that the eternal element in you (the Trinity just mentioned), which is your true *Self*, cannot have any beginning or end. It seems easy to say, but not so easy to live. Meditate again about this axiom in full peace of mind and clarity of consciousness and finally you *will know IT*, as did and do others on the Path. Therefore, nothing, absolutely nothing, can change your *true core*, cannot add to or subtract anything from it. All yogas, holy exercises, occult methods and so on operate *only on the veils* enveloping the *Self*, but *never on IT ! IT cannot be either subject or object, for IT alone is*. All other things are shadows in time and space.

If you want to be successful on the Path, do not read ahead until you understand this truth within you, without any trace of doubt.

*   *   *   *

From the title of this chapter we see that the first preparatory step to our aim is—*Justice*, applied at all times and in everything. Again, it is easier to say than to realize.

Firstly, justice should be practised in our physical activities. Beginning with our own physical tool, the body, we must practise justice in our environment. The body must perform its functions harmoniously, for then it will not distract us from our supreme Aim.

At this point someone may say that he is Spirit-Self and not the body, and therefore would not like to occupy himself with any mayavic functions (care of the body in the sense just used). It all sounds very nice, but reality is not so. Who dares to pronounce such a sentence, which in its deepest meaning is absolutely true? Are you practically, here and now, really the pure Spirit? Are you independent of your body? Will your consciousness really not be affected by a racking toothache, fever, crippling rheumatism and similar conditions? Will you be unaffected by bad news about your family, finances, or work? Only if under such circumstances you can truthfully answer 'No!' are you independent of all outer conditions, thereby being not less than a Jivanmukta, a Reintegrated One, briefly, a perfect Liberated Being. But in that case you will not read this book, or any other.

Therefore, I have to presume that you are not yet so far advanced, and I will continue.

We must be, as was already said, just to our body, giving it what it really needs, no more, no less. If you do so, you will see that average people usually overburden their bodies with excess of food and drink. This makes the shell too clumsy for our purpose, disobedient and requiring too much attention.

Therefore, work out the best standards for food, sleep, movement and work for yourself. I have never heard of anyone reaching Samadhi who ate the flesh of other creatures (at least, of warm-blooded ones), or was a drunkard or addict of harmful habits, drugs, and so on. This is the first practical suggestion for each earnest

51

student. Occultists, who never identify themselves with their bodies, consider their physical counterpart as a temporary instrument, given to them for the fulfilment of certain tasks. If the instrument is wrongly treated it cannot possibly give good service. Therefore our *justice* to the physical shell and the surrounding world should be, to give them exactly the measured and necessary amount of attention and material means. Not more nor less !

Allow the body only the needed quantity of everything: food, rest, exercise, movement, natural sports such as walking, and swimming (if you like it). If all this might appear to be terribly boring and impossible to an average man because of his identification with the physical body, it will come with much less effort to an advanced occultist, and this is quite understandable. If you cannot suppress unnecessary and harmful habits, that is only because the body rules over you. There is no other explanation. But a man who is 'inwardly' strong does not permit such degradation. For him it is the same as if his boots were ordering him where to walk. Samadhi is for those who master their bodies, and not for the enslaved.

As a very effective means for the systematic cleansing of impurities from the body, some occultists recommend the taking of Turkish baths, at least once weekly. The writer agrees with this, as he has personally had confirmatory experience with these baths, and has noted the considerable benefit derived from them. But not less than two hours should elapse after a meal before taking a Turkish bath.

However, this kind of bath should not be confused with the different *steam* types known as Sauna, Russian baths, and so on, which can easily affect not-so-strong hearts. The Turkish system uses only *dry heat*, which is harmless for everyone.

Think about all this before trying to engage yourself on the Sublime Path.

The *second* application of the Law of Justice will concern that of the emotional (or astral) body and world. It is a much more complicated and difficult task, being a natural development of the first one. The *third* will deal with just the mind and its plane. Here is an important warning: do not think that these things should be taken strictly in *turn*, that is, first the physical body, then the astral and finally the mental. It would be a great mistake, because of the immense amount of time required for such a slow process. The Master Maharshi confirmed this when a visitor quoted the old Roman proverb: *Mens sana in corpore sano* (a healthy spirit in a healthy body), meaning that allegedly we should *first* acquire and then maintain a strong physical shell, and afterwards begin to try for higher things. The Sage answered with a smile: '*In such a case there would be never ending care of the body.*'

By this he meant the absorbing care which does not allow a man any true evolutionary activities, as is the case with human nature, to care for that which, according to our present point of view, is most important and dear to us. No, our efforts must be performed *simultaneously* in all three directions, or, in other words, on all the three planes of existence. Only then can we expect a harmonious development and maintenance of our tools, which finally sets us free from all of them—in Samadhi.

It is only because of the impossibility of expounding this question other than in sequence, that you read these instructions as if divided into three parts, following one after another.

So, the principle of justice applied to the *astral* means the rational control of its vibrations. Under the term 'vibrations' in different planes, we accept the functioning of the consciousness in those planes. In short it is: a refusal to allow any disharmonious (or evil) movements to occur in our emotions and feelings. If we look closer at this rule, we will discover an *ordinary moral code* beneath it, but extended and subtilized to the utmost limits of possibility. On broad lines, negative vibrations (details of which are left to the student to establish for himself, as it is easy and rather individual work) are: feelings of anger, fear, jealousy, envy, hatred, sensuality, grief, despair, and all the derivatives of this unholy litany. They must not take any part in your astral life. And what of the so-called 'desirable' emotions like love, courage, serenity, purity of feeling, and so on? *Do not worry about them!* Human nature is so arranged that there cannot be any vacuum in the three worlds, in which we normally live, *until Samadhi is reached.*

For Samadhi is virtually the rejection and transcending of all the three. By lack of vacuum is meant, that instead of the expelled *negative*, astral vibrations, there must come positive ones. How can this be? Simply test it on yourself! If you destroy hatred in you (not only forget, but really destroy without any possibility of its revival) love will come as a result. This is the *law*. And so it follows with all emotions. Someone may protest: instead of the destroyed hatred, indifference might simply arise. Not so! Because here the 'indifference' would again mean a negative attitude, enclosing you in the vicious and narrow circle of your ego, that primordial enemy of every expansion of consciousness.

Do not confuse *indifference* with *non-attachment*, which is the attribute of great souls. When I sat at the feet of the Master, I never saw any trace of indifference on his wonderful face, but only that sublime freedom of full attainment, penetrated by divine spiritual compassion, which radiated from him and which melted the hard outer shells round the hearts of men.

Again, the effort of annihilation of some sort of negative vibrations in your astral or mental also means a subconscious process of purification, technically, of the removal of some more veils, which cover the immortal, eternal, and perfect *core* of every being. So how could something wrong slip into you if there is no entrance for it remaining in you?

Before you reach your aim, you will have to become quite a good psychologist, dealing with the living manifestations in you and in your brothers—the men as well as the animals around you. But this does not mean any theoretical, borrowed or accepted scholastic exposition of a system, of which many are still present in the world of today. The concocted 'psychological systems' made by those who are not even masters of their own lives, are useless to you. Your practical psychology must be *your own*, which you learn during the time of preparatory study such as this. True psychology is, and can be, only that which we find in the depths of our own being-consciousness, if we can dive into those depths.

To return to the annihilation of negative astral vibrations, the student will surely understand, that this work cannot be performed 'with bare hands'. Yes, we need a good, sharp tool for it, and this is none other than the power, well known to us, of concentration, based on the will-power possessed. This is the pivot and the fulcrum of all our endeavours. It is like matriculation for a university course. This should never be forgotten. If you wish to know the last steps preceding Samadhi, then realize that they are just the *special, silent use of concentration*, which permits the stoppage of all vibrations belonging to the three manifested worlds. Those who have reached this point will know what I mean. And it is a great spiritual joy to know about other fellow-travellers, who arrive, after immeasurable toil, at the same eternal *'point'*, beyond which there is nothing more to attain. To know, that within some physical forms (How few in this epoch!) the imperishable, eternal Light is already kindling, and that then there is realized the Life, beyond all death and suffering, the Life extending beyond all, for it *is*—the *Whole*.

About fifty years ago a Sage in far-off India began his sublime work, reminding humanity of its forgotten heritage, the eternal freedom of realized *Self* in man.

A man, who not seeking any fame, glory or advertising, sat through his long life in the deep, continuous state of supreme Samadhi, unhindered by his apparently 'normal' life. He moved, spoke, ate and slept, without abandoning even for a second his *Sahaja Nirvikalpa Samadhi*, attainable only by the perfect Master-Men. Mystery covers such glory of Attainment, for all we can hope to reach now and probably for many, many lives ahead, is the *Kevala Nirvikalpa Samadhi*. Where lies the difference between these almost synonymous terms? In the first words of these expressions, *Sahaja* means *uninterrupted, perennial, unbroken*, while *Kevala, temporary* and *limited*. The difference seems to be just in the 'quantity' and not the 'quality', and the Master Maharshi apparently supported this idea. When speaking about the eternal and temporary Samadhis he pointed out, that it is the mind, which makes the whole difference. If it is completely 'dead' (the Master's own expression), then Samadhi extends to everything in both waking and sleeping states, as well as after the abandonment of the physical body at death.

If the mind—as is the case with all of us—is only temporarily dominated and compelled to silence, it will return to its former activities, as the inner power in such a man does not suffice for the abandoning of everything relative, and for not taking an interest in these matters (relativity): just like a plane, which can remain in the air for only as long as it has sufficient fuel.

Those who have experienced Samadhi know that the words of the Master are true in all their simplicity. After being in Samadhi for some minutes (sometimes even hours), we are compelled to return. There is a *Power* which orders that return, and nothing can resist it. I can only recommend students to read the works of Sri Ramana Maharshi in the original English translations, which are readily available from his former Ashram in Tiruvannamalai, South India.

*   *   *   *

The most comprehensible and understandable scheme of our astral behaviour can be obtained from the following conception. Imagine your emotional activities as a kind of radiation, streaming from yourself to the outer world. You know that in physics there are different kinds of radiations. Some like, say, sunlight are beneficial, others, like those of rare metals (e.g. Strontium 90), are harmful and may cause disease or even death. If you indulge in your negative astral feelings like those enumerated at the beginning of this chapter, then you poison the astral atmosphere round you, damaging the astrosomes of your surroundings, and further still, infecting them, like a contagious sickness, thus forcing them to accept and, consequently later, to emit similar vibrations. Do you understand the injustice of which you are guilty in such a case?

If you act oppositely, that is, you radiate full peace and other positive feelings, then you add your astral activities to the reservoir of healthy vibrations, thereby exercising an evolutionary influence on your environment. There is no action without reaction, and there are no results without a cause. These two axioms should always be kept before the inner sight of every aspirant to higher consciousness. Our unsympathetic feelings directed towards our neighbours create similar ones in them. It is a very well known fact that human beings are very susceptible to such emotions, especially those created 'instinctively'. For example, you may enter a train or tram, where there are no vacant seats, but if some passengers sat a little closer together, room could be found for another traveller.

. You see this, but nobody moves. An average man will feel inner indignation against the selfish passengers. In the astral light this can be observed as livid streams, with, say, a reddish lining. But it is not important. What really counts, is the creation of negative, poisonous currents of energy by the unwise person. This is 'illegal' from our point of view, and therefore it is a break in astral justice.

Examples could be cited 'ad infinitum', but it is the business of the student, not of the writer, bound as he is by space limitations in a book. None of the negative vibrations created by us are justifiable. It may be understandable that sometimes we have hard feelings against those who do evil to us, as we believe; but nevertheless, it is unjust from the spiritual point of view. How can we reach spiritual consciousness—Samadhi—if we break spiritual laws? Between spiritual and material justice there is an abyss, over which there never was, is, or will be a *bridge*. Examples? Well, Christ prayed for His executioners; He advised us to turn the other cheek when we are hit on one; He further told us what might easily be beyond our understanding: 'Do not resist evil.' The Maharshi, robbed and beaten by thieves, while having the full possibility of preventing it, since his disciples, who were with him that night, were more numerous and stronger than the assailants, ordered them *not to resist* and turned his right side to the blows, when the left had already been struck. As spiritual truths are inaccessible to reasoning, I leave the explanation to the student's own intuition, for it is intuition which presents the proper instrument for spiritual cognition and enlightenment.

Even magicians know that the best defence against invultuation and other hostile actions on the astral plane, is sincere and unconditional forgiveness and prayers for the offender.

* * * *

There remains the *third* kind of attitude necessary for those who prepare themselves for the Superconsciousness. Of course, it is mental culture, the mental justice in us, just as it was with the physical and astral ones.

With thoughts as the mental products, there are different standards. Right, or just, thinking has several attributes, which, in brief, are as follow:

(1) Concentration, that is, lack of dissipation of one's thinking processes. This means, that when we are thinking about, say, an apple we should not mix it up with lemons, pears and other fruit. The sense of this example should be clear to us. If we have to place a simple object before our mind's screen, it must be the only one in the focus of our concentration. Deviations in the direction of affinities of objects should be excluded. When we need to think about our watch, only *its picture* should be before our sight, and thought should not extend itself to the makers of the watch, its qualities, value, and so on. This is because, if we extend the field of our concentration, the process becomes a meditation or deliberation about the object's qualities and other details, which is beyond our purpose and therefore a sheer distortion of concentration. We have to learn to think about very simple things, and only then will we show ourselves mature enough for more complicated problems connected with the necessary art of meditation, which is the basis for Samadhi.

The rule is: think at a given time about only *one* object, no matter to which realm it belongs. Then the more complicated processes in your mind will be easy to control and dominate. Without abiding by this rule, your mind will for ever remain a powerless and disobedient thing. As you are supposed to study another basic work—*Concentration*—before reading this book, I have little more to add.

(2) Every problem should be presented clearly to your mind, that is, do not allow any misty, indefinite forms to arise in your mental and no vague ideas dare be admitted. If the subject is not clear enough, concentrate your attention on it until you 'see' it clearly.

(3) A most important moment in 'right thinking' as preparation for Samadhi, is acquired by the habit of concentration, to consider all mental processes arising in the mind as something *apart* from yourself, which can be, and is separated from your I-core. It is a *condition* 'sine qua non'. You will never reach Samadhi while identifying yourself with the mind, just as was the case with your feelings. It is the greatest injustice inflicted on your *Self*, when you do not get rid of the involutionary habit (acquired in so many previous incarnations), of confounding the tools with the master using them. This basic separation on the occult way is again

achieved by the development of the ability of practical concentration, which leads to domination of the mind's functions.

Then we see, that the machine and the operator cannot be one. On religious paths the same is supposed to be achieved by 'renunciation of one's own will', as practised in monasteries and convents. It is a considerably long way, and the novice usually does not know that which you are studying in this chapter. He has to believe unconditionally in the wisdom of his prior, who gives him none or very few psychological explanations connected with the rules enforced in monasteries.

Obedience to the spiritual leader in such cases is the cardinal condition in religious orders of all denominations, where these orders still exist. In other words, in those denominations in which there is still given the opportunity for advancement to those of the faithful, who feel that their vocation is to enter such an order and dedicate their lives to its service.

But a few more energetic people need different paths, like those discussed in this book, which give more scientific and faster access to the aim.

(4) Justice in discrimination concerning the influence of the environment and other men on the aspirant, is necessarily a foremost mental virtue for him. Often we are disappointed in human unfriendliness, sometimes even animosity, which happens when we are treading the Path. Occasionally I hear otherwise quite able students say: 'All my efforts are directed to maintaining peace in myself and with the world. In spite of this, and without any cause from my side, I experience all kinds of unfairness and hostility. Where then lies justice?'

The answer may be twofold.

(a) *For your mind* it will be: man usually does not know his past beyond his present incarnation. So, even if in this life he seems to be correct in his attitude towards the world (which is very hard to establish properly), retaliations can come as a result of past existences, and it is usually so.

(b) *For your spirit*, the solution to this controversial problem will be the answer given in similar circumstances by Thomas à Kempis to his subordinate monks in his *Imitation of Christ* (Book 2, Chapter 1).

'Christ also was despised by men in the world, and in His greatest need He was, by His acquaintance and His friends, forsaken amidst insults . . .

'Christ had enemies and detractors, and wouldst thou have all to be thy friends and benefactors?

'Whence shall thy patience be crowned, if thou meet with no adversity?'

This can be considered as most enlightening for those able to look into the depths of things with spiritual insight.

(5) Avoid verbalization at any price. Learn to think, when you are compelled to, or when you meditate or try to solve a complicated problem, without forming words and repeating them in your mind. The Great Rishi Ramana, the most eminent authority on spiritual psychology, called words 'the great-grandsons of truth' and by this emphasized the inadequacy of speech for research into one's true Self. Thinking without words and concrete images belongs to individuals who are fairly advanced in the control of their minds. It is also one of the preconditions leading to Samadhi. It cannot be achieved without well-directed efforts (see *Concentration*, Part III).

(6) Pacify your mind, that is, do not emit any hastily concocted restless thoughts. They could be unjust to your environment, influencing it adversely, and this then means another hindrance for you on your Path.

(7) Learn to be just in your thoughts about other men. If it is necessary to judge them, always do it impartially as if standing apart from yourself and looking dispassionately, with the same eye, on both them and yourself. If you cease to be enamoured of your body, this attitude will be established in you without much inner struggle. Take inspiration from the unselfishness of the Spiritual Masters and see how perfect they were.

Read the lives of saints and great Teachers of humanity, for this undoubtedly has an incontestable and ennobling influence on a man's psyche. For those who have a deeply subtle, spiritual attitude, St John's Gospel will prove to be an inexhaustible source of a fine, uplifting force. Especially the last sermons of the Son of Man to His disciples, which are full of mystical light.

A great occultist and keen philosopher, the late Professor G. O. Mebes, of the former Imperial University of St Petersburg (see my *Tarot*), says: 'Make the best use of your incarnations, for they are not given to you without any meaning, or for nothing!'

Ages ago the word 'good' was often substituted by '*just*'. In His dramatic last prayer, before being delivered into the hands of His executioners, the Teacher addressed God as: '*O Just Father!*'

It is synonymous with all the other attributes possessed by the Supreme. The reflection of Justice in your heart is a condition for any successful attempt to reach the *kingdom*, which we now call 'Samadhi'.

Chapter IX

The Building of the Inner Sanctuary

Verse 138: 'O disciple, with mind under control, directly
perceive this, the *atman* in thyself as—"this I am"—
through the tranquillity of *buddhi* cross the shoreless sea
of changeful existence, whose billows are birth and death,
and accomplish thy end, resting firmly in the form of
Brahman.'

Verse 412: 'Having brought the *antahkarana* (mind) to rest,
in the true self, you should perceive it, whose glory is
indestructible; with assiduous efforts sever the bondage
tainted by the smell of conditioned existence, and render
fruitful your manhood.'

IN the foregoing chapter we learned about the right attitude in the
three manifested worlds, necessary for the first approach to Superconsciousness—Samadhi. From this we can realize that Samadhi cannot be achieved by unripe human beings, simply because they do not
know and do not wish to know anything about it, since they are
absorbed in the lower worlds, not as free travellers, but as ones deeply
attached and enslaved by the false charm of the gross vibrations of
material life. And finally, because of their heavy karmas they cannot
be placed in conditions appropriate for entrance on to the Path.
Nothing can help them except *time*, incessantly flowing and gradually correcting their faults for the price of suffering.

Christ referred to this inert majority in different terms. Once He
said: 'Let the dead bury their dead.' But for those around Him who
were more advanced He advised: 'Come ye after me. . . .' 'They have
eyes and they see not; they have ears and they hear not.'

It was given to me to observe a striking example with my own
eyes. About ten years ago, when, for long months I sat at the feet of
the Master, trying to absorb his Light and take the greatest profit
from the living Presence, thousands of people came in the same
period to get the Darshan of the Sage. Every one of them was im-
pressed by the spiritual magnitude, purity and wisdom of the departing Rishi. They came and they left in a few days, subsequently forgetting their lofty moments at Maharshi's feet.

But a few remained faithful. In the course of time they deepened the direct influence exercised on them by the Master, and when he left this earth, they retained the *golden thread* for ever.

We know from history, that even the most powerful manifestations of the Spirit, incarnate in a given period, on this planet, have never been able to convert or enlighten all men alive at the time. On the contrary, only a small minority has ever been ripe enough to accept the Message and to 'bear fruit', as Christ told us.

No miracles, cures or other manifestations of a supernatural character are able to speak to such underdeveloped people, still deeply merged in the illusion of their materialistic egoism. All depends upon our inner ripeness and contents.

Another preparation for obtaining the Superconsciousness in us is a process which we call 'the Building of the Inner Sanctuary'. This means to reach, through well-directed meditation, appropriate way of life and incessant effort, the unruffled depth in our consciousness, unattainable for any lower (or evil) vibrations. There must be a point in us, where peace reigns supreme, and where we will have our last refuge, amongst the storms of our karmas, which rage around our short, but strenuous Path.

This mystical, but how real, inner point can be found, and one can establish oneself in it, albeit temporarily, as many have done. It is important not to speak about It, but to discover It. And here, often lies a tragedy: people who have some flashes of intuition may know about the necessity of building in themselves now, that inner sanctuary, as we will call it, but they lack the techniques or will-power, sometimes both. Here we may see the overwhelming importance of realization, and not just a theoretical grasp of things.

Old proverbs usually show amazing wisdom of life, and I would like to quote one of them:

'The way to hell is paved with good intentions.'

Of course, only with *unrealized intentions*. Many years ago, when I still indulged (also 'with good intentions') in discussions with people who only talked, but lacked the qualities to prove what they professed, I had the opportunity to note the truth referred to in this old proverb. But dissipation and empty verbal deliberations are rather obstacles and not a help to gaining Samadhi.

Therefore, these things have to be stopped. If you begin to build the inner sanctuary in you, as a forerunner, or 'outer court' for the Superconsciousness, the grace of those who are already establishing themselves in this invisible temple of the soul will be granted to you.

They will meet you in due time, in person or by correspondence, this is not essential. But then you will know experimentally, that beyond egoistic, emotional, economic, religious, social, racial and political battles taking place on the outer side of things (in other words, in the world), there is a sure port of ineffable peace, where you can cast your anchor (that is, the mind) and so find the rest, for which dream, toil and strive all beings through their sufferings.

I mentioned that 'techniques' are needed for the building of the inner sanctuary in us, just as for a home of bricks and mortar. Therefore I am obliged to point them out. They are amazingly simple, almost as simple as the Truth itself, and inaccessible to many just because of that simplicity, which transcends the limits of the untrained and unsubdued mind. We still do not know much about our mind, the instrument of everyday life, which can be made an instrument of Attainment. This has been widely explained in *Concentration*.

We cannot do much better than take as the fundamentals for our Inner Sanctuary, the three commandments of the Lord Buddha, given in order to regulate man's inner life, in the simplest way, without engaging the many cogs of the mind. I quote them from *In Days of Great Peace*:

(1) Cease doing evil;
(2) Learn to do good;
(3) Purify your own heart.

An immensity of understanding, effort and realization is embodied in these brief sentences, and a certain degree of inner ripeness is necessary in order to see them through. The unripe person will pass over them, thinking that they are only theoretical hints, when in reality they are the way of life for many incarnations, depending upon the starting point and development of the seeker.

Such a person will prefer to search for voluminous books and thousands of mentally smooth words, which ingeniously embroider a pattern round their spiritual emptiness and uselessness. This is a very sad truth. The creators of these volumes were only slaves of their own minds; but the Sanctuary which we are seeking to build is a dwelling for *free beings*, who rule over their minds and emotions.

These commandments have no value apart from their practice, and they are destined not to become dissected by verbalizing, superficial minds, but—*to be lived*. And so it is with all the jewels of Truth given to us by the Great Teachers. The foundation of the Inner Sanctuary will be laid by you on just that day, when you refuse to do evil any more. When this is done, the walls will be much easier to erect, that is *to learn to do good*. These two stages will deal with your karma, allowing you to advance without any catastrophe in the astral and mental planes. And no entity in this vast universe has been able to escape or defy this law. Look at the disciples of the true Masters: they are always active according to their Master's line and spiritual legacy. Why do they act so? There are many good reasons for this.

Firstly, they pay the debt which they contracted on receiving initiation and help, and purification of their subtle vehicles (astral and mental) from the Master. This repayment invariably brings the *grace* of the Teacher. Although genuine disciples are conscious of the impossibility of repaying *all* that they receive and the benefits bestowed on them, they do their best and cease to worry about the rest. No other way exists.

Secondly, while working along their Master's lines, they learn His work in advance, knowing that there will come a day, when they too will have to carry the full burden of the *cross* on their shoulders, as every Master has done.

Thirdly, the last part of the Sanctuary—its roof as we may say— which is the *purification of one's heart*, can be built only when the first two have been erected, and slavery to karma brought to an end.

These three commandments of the Buddha are in relativity as a keen student will certainly see, for there is still 'good and 'evil', there is still effort and action. But who could take profit from the 'absolute' commandments, if such could ever exist? Only the *Perfect One*, who has transcended all relativity in himself. But does such a *One* need any commandments or lessons?

On the other hand, it is impossible to inculcate the immaterial, the absolute into a human being, still not fully developed. The Teachers know the world and the conditions in it very well and they act according to their wisdom.

There are also other kinds of keys to the antechamber of Samadhi. But we agreed, although without exchanging words, to speak in this book only about the most practical things and methods, concentrating on them as it became convenient, so as to give realizable instructions, while not adding any mental ballast, the scar of which already burdens our minds, as an inheritance from former experiences and lives. Also, very inquisitive seekers can find different guideposts in the words of other Teachers, providing they do not lack the ability to sense the subtle perfume of Truth, and thereby find its source.

Such people may find interest in the exposition of the two paths to Achievement, that of the *mind* and the *heart*, spoken of in Chapters VIII and IX respectively, of *Concentration*.

The Roman Emperor Titus, a philosopher, and a good man when

on the throne, used to say, that 'lost is the day when one does not perform a good deed'. The realization of the three commandments of the Buddha should start with just this 'not losing of a day'.

The power which will sustain you in your decision to follow this maxim will grow proportionally to your endurance. This *power* cannot be described but it can, and must, be felt and known. One of its attributes which can be mentioned is that: '*it is at once both inside and outside of us.*'

Another means leading to the establishment of the Inner Sanctuary in us is the practising of the well-known Eastern rule, called in Hindu Sacred books—*Ahimsa*, or harmlessness. We should not hurt anybody or bring any suffering into the world by our actions. It is also a very broad rule, and the exclusion of any harm in our deeds needs a lot of practical philosophy and concentration in life, plus the ability of penetrating observation.

There is a nasty element in us, which incites us to injurious speech, to the pin-pricking of our fellow men, without any reason or even aim. Sometimes people like to be sarcastic, to have stinging tongues. We cannot be occupied with the building of the inner temple, as mentioned before, and at the same time spread negative feelings, thoughts, speech and deeds around us. Why is this so? Very simple ! These negative things are the ugly manifestations of the *ego*, that bulwark of separateness, of that great *lie*, which led, as occultists say, to the downfall of man and to his present degradation. But Samadhi is just the full and realized *negation* of that illusory separateness, based essentially on the transcending of the mind, which is the last bastion of egoism. Superconsciousness is as incompatible with ego-ridden slavery as is fire mixed with water. This will be quite clear at the end of this book, when attempts will be made to translate the experiences of Samadhi into human language.

All this must be clearly understood, and the student should not have any dreamy imagination, that he may be able to reach true Samadhi and still remain a slave to his vices and their paramount ruler—*egoism*, or the inner belief in his separate existence. All his long life he can repeat the verses of Sankaracharya or Maharshi, and the sayings of Christ or Buddha, to which is traditionally ascribed, the power to lift human consciousness beyond its present level, and he will still be far off true Samadhi, if materialistic egoism is his over-lord. This is the cause of the fact, that only Perfect Men (Masters), who have no trace of separateness in them, can enjoy the *Sahaja* (Perennial) *Nirvikalpa* (Formless) Samadhi.

And it is just the amount of the great illusion (Maya) of egoism, still existing in us in a hidden state, which does not allow us to reach the *Sahaja*, but only the *Kevala*, that is, temporary flights into the Superconsciousness of the future.

Nothing can change this fact, and it remains for us, if we are reasonable, evolutionary beings, to try *to reduce* the intervals between these flights as much as possible, and so lengthen our soaring in the Truth of Spirit.

Those who are lucky enough to preserve a genuine faith and love in the Master of Masters,[1] can be greatly helped in the building of their Inner Sanctuary by a *Gnostic prayer*, which is still present in the mystical tradition of one of the ancient churches.

It can be used as an uplifting and purifying meditation throughout the lifetime, as well as in one's last hour.

'To Thy last supper let me be allowed today, O Son of God!
For neither will I betray any secret to Thine enemies,
Nor will I give Thee a kiss like Judas,
But like the thief I pray unto Thee:
Remember me O Lord, when coming into Thy Kingdom!'

The comments, if any are needed, can be found only in your own heart.

When practising these meditations and theurgic formulas (or prayers), the student usually experiences a definite wave of inner elation, or happiness of a subtle kind, and so-called temporary 'dematerialization', which here means the turning of the attention to the higher, non-perishable and non-egoistic, but spiritual conceptions, then born in the consciousness.

Moreover, one may then be even fully aware that these are possibly just the best moments in life, and one would not exchange them for any physical or everyday attractions and boons.

Well, why then are there so many failures? Simply because men, who experience that inner bliss, are too apt to forget it in the ever-flowing turmoil and petty pleasures or desires of the material, mortal life. *This forgetfulness is fatal*, for it is the only true cause and factor which bans us from the Path and Attainment. This statement must be meditated upon according to one's personal life, until you become firmly convinced of its truthfulness. When this happens, you may see the *enemy* clearer and so be better able to fight him.

Those who have succeeded are called—depending upon their

---

[1] This expression was used by both Sri Maharshi and P. Sédir.

degree of advancement—saints or true yogis, and when they are finishing the Path, *Masters* or Perfect Men.

Therefore the constant admonitions by Masters to their disciples are always uniform:

> 'Never forget, but incessantly and systematically practise your meditations and prayers, without omitting to memorize their blissful influence on yourself. Constantly compare them with the dark conditions of the unconscious life, as led by the majority of your brethren. Otherwise you might easily forget what should not be forgotten, and to remember it only in your last hour, but then it is too late to fight the visions and nightmares of a frustrated life, of a spiritually barren incarnation, bringing new suffering and toil for the future.'

This is also one of the causes which make men shun death so much.

* * * *

Finally, the Sanctuary in us, when erected, means that our fulcrum no longer lies in the visible and tangible things, accessible to our senses. It means, that our better part, which we consider to be closest to our *Core* or *Self*—is in another, happier world, more pure, beautiful and real, because of its comparative permanency. This is a result of our having built it by applying purity, inner harmony and that perennial element in us, which is hidden behind every spark of manifested life.

Then the temple is ready to receive the *light of Samadhi*.

Sometimes, those ripe enough to use properly the *mystical prayer* mentioned in this chapter, have immediate and wonderful experiences as a result. Feelings of immense bliss penetrate them; tears often stream profusely; the beating of their hearts becomes as it does in a rapture, and even speech dies on their lips. Know that this is the sign that the golden *door* is ready to open for you. Persevere and you will enter into the *temple* built by your own efforts and consecrated by the almighty *Spirit*.

Chapter x

The World and the 'I'

Verse 432: 'Though existing in this body which is like a shadow, to be yet devoid of egotism and the consciousness of possession is the characteristic of a *jivanmukta*.'

Verse 462: 'When is the reality of what is supposed and whence is the origin of unreality? Whence is then destruction of what is not born? Whence is there *prarabdha* of what is unreal?'

A S you can see, Samadhi requires a lot of changes in our attitude and psychology. I am giving them in this work on broad lines which, if assimilated, dispense with details, as they will be worked out by the individual consciousness of the student.

These lines come to us in an unusual way, because, only from Samadhi, can they be seen as relative qualities gathered just below the level of Samadhi in the aspirant's consciousness.

From this comes the assertion, that because certain attitudes can be recognized as forerunners of Samadhi, they should therefore be practised by those who have not yet experienced the Superconsciousness, in order to serve as helpful steps leading to the summit. The whole of Part II of this work is composed of just these steps.

Now we will occupy ourselves with the cardinal problem of our I and the outer world, in so far as these two terms still have meaning for us. This problem is for ever solved in Samadhi, beyond all doubts and queries, simply because duality is unthinkable and impossible in that transcendent state.

Otherwise, it is the chief condition of Samadhi, that in the 'Fourth State' (see *Concentration*) there is neither I nor *non-I*, but only the nonpolarized Reality, indivisible and beyond subject and object. In our 'normal' waking state the basic duality prevails, and the binary: I and *non-I* (or the outer world) remains. First let us briefly analyse what is that I, in the 'normal' consciousness of the average man.

We cannot speak about any advanced forms of I until we are fully aware of what an ordinary human I—EGO is.

Sit quietly, preferably in solitude, and ask yourself: 'Who am I just at this moment?' For a while reject all your theories and teachings—if you are somewhat acquainted with certain conceptions of the superior forms of *I*—because you have to begin with your actual and real experience of yourself, and not with any theory, no matter how acceptable, lofty and true it may be for you at this time. A bird starts its flight by first pushing its body away from the earth by a forceful rebounding with its legs, but first of all, those legs have to find a firm support on the hard surface. Perhaps this simple simile will be helpful for you in your meditation at this moment.

So, what constitutes ourselves when we are sitting and trying to approach the closest possible meaning of our *I*, for you cannot operate with anything other than your own consciousness?

Think about this until you accept it as expressing your own inner truth. I speak deliberately about *your I* for we are not able to use anything else apart from our own consciousness. Of course, when you solve the problem for yourself then you will be in a position to understand something more about the other *I*'s, which fill the world round you. These *other I*'s do not really exist, but until Samadhi is reached, this illusion remains. '*Samadhi alone can reveal the truth,*' said the Maharshi.

In our process of meditation and self-analysis we inevitably come to certain answers, which can be anticipated here. These are:

(a) I am this 'something' which sits and meditates about Itself.

(b) Different thoughts come to me from outer space, but I try to filter them, accepting only those which are related to my present problem—my everyday I.

(c) Also I actually have the feeling of my physical body, but as I know from foregoing chapters, it is too far from my real I to be considered in this meditation.

(d) The ability to think, and—what is of greatest importance—to filter and to select my thoughts, allowing only those necessary to enter into the magic circle of my consciousness, is certainly an attribute of my I.

(e) Therefore, I am not these mental functions in any way whatsoever.

(f) From this real conception comes another, again of cardinal value for every student: I cannot say that I am *This* or *That*, for it is only mental imagination, a product, a thing, and not the I, which observes and actually meditates about them.

(g) Therefore I must finish all hopeless efforts to find myself amongst things, no matter how eminent or even transcendent they may appear to me to be. The fact that my consciousness is able to deal with them makes only objects of them, but not the subject itself.

(h) Consequently, all I am to find of my I now, is *That* which thinks
and feels, and which has many properties and other things. But
it is *That* which all these things cannot have in themselves. This
should end our search for a while, that search which will be the
basis for establishing our relations with all the things and forces
apart from us, that is the world, as we are accustomed to call this
'collection'.

What relation has it to us?

(1) Firstly, objects apart from our own body, over which we have
certain authority, including all that we see, hear, touch, and so
on, are rejected by us as being *non-I*, because they cannot help
us much.

(2) Apart from (1) above, there are some more interesting things
which may affect us. These are the *I*'s which are supposed to be
like us, but are separated from our *I* by their visible (and invisible)
bodies. In them is also a similar degree of consciousness-life, about
the contents of which we can only guess with greater or less
probability.

(3) These incarnate consciousnesses—*I*'s, are the active part of the
world surrounding us, of our *non-I*.

*　　*　　*　　*

These examples of basic meditations will suffice, if practised with
steadiness, until the subject becomes clear to us. This great problem
of *man* and the universe surrounding him has been the theme of
many philosophical theories, but here we need only a few concrete
and immediately workable individual conceptions. At this point the
student will do well if he practises both series of meditations and tries
to obtain some definite conclusions from them. It is always so in-
tensely individual—as it should be—that I would not undertake any
unnecessary and hopeless task such as trying to suggest to, or impress
on you my own solution, which I too had to find at some time in the
past. I hope you will understand that this is only right at this stage
and at this time. Therefore, we will now pass on to logical approaches,
which can be applied to everyone, without binding his or her initia-
tive, while helping to develop the same.

There are two known mental conceptions. The first one is that we
are dependent upon the world, being only a part of it and being conditioned by it. In this case the binary (*part* and *whole*) still continues
to exist, and it is hard to foresee any possible neutralization of it (that
is, solution for it). All we can say is that here the *Whole* seems to
possess its own life, proceeding on many lines (currents) above and
beyond our own line.

Sometimes it has a similar direction to ours and then it *co-operates* with, or helps us, as some people like to say. Then it is good for us. But often things are just the opposite. And then the forces of the world move in vastly different directions from ours, which they cross and even damage.

Then they are *evil*, and not good for us. In our lives we try to balance the influence of the outer world on us, to restrict (as only we can) the opposite currents, and to join the co-operative ones.

Sometimes we succeed, and then we are happy for a time; often we cannot control things as we wish, and then we live unhappily.

On this level, no permanent solution of the binary has been found, when individualities (egos) fight between themselves. All that we can do for our present purpose is to note the fact.

The second conception is, that we are virtually independent of the outer world. If this is realized, then great things will occur in our lives. One then refuses to yield to the temptations and threats of the world, because then one's attitude can best be defined by the words of a Great Teacher of humanity: '*Be in the world but not of it.*' This means that man should not be bound by outer conditions as his true being is far beyond all of them. Analyse now what your position is.

Independence of the world is achieved when events have no power over our moods and states of mind. Bad news, physical shocks or disease, a successful endeavour, robust health, all these things which come from the outer world become just like moving pictures in a cinema. We look at them, but we know that they are only illusory reflections of the actor's performance, recorded on a film and then projected on a cold and lifeless screen. Is it not so with our existence here? Some power breathed life into our bodies, which without that breath become the same dust, from which they arose. Many people have complained that the conditions of the outer world make any deeper inner insight impossible for them. 'I simply have not time for it,' they say. 'I have all my time taken up with the problems of "real" life and nothing left for any spiritual aspirations.' Here lies the foremost difficulty and misunderstanding. The basis is, of course, the identification with their bodies by such people. It is just the body which underlies these different conditions, but not the invisible man, independent (at least he should be so if sufficiently advanced) of his perishable shells. The misunderstanding lies in the widespread conviction, that any earnest inner work, concentration or meditation is possible only in almost hermit-like conditions, with actually nothing to do apart from deliberation and contemplation. In actuality such karmic conditions usually come only to the very ripe souls who have already passed through most earthly tribulations, and who have transferred their consciousness to solid foundations. If an unripe man could get the karma of such an advanced person, he would be most unhappy and bored. He would struggle fiercely to get into a 'more real and interesting environment'. While a hermit or occultist abides quietly and meditates happily, the 'worldly man' has no intention to do anything of the kind. He tries to merge into the vortex of the common life.

To know this will make your decisions easier and more appropriate. But a man who enters on the Path has a different attitude towards the world. He knows that he has to live among those whom the infallible karma (created by himself, and no one else) puts in his way in the given incarnation. And he also knows that in order to gain conditions belonging to highly developed souls, he must fight imperfections in himself, purify the accounts of his karma, and progressively work on his mind and emotions, to acquire the principal virtue, that is, *right concentration*. But the latter can be performed even without any special system being brought into play. This statement might sound astonishing coming from the author who wrote a book entitled *Concentration*; but it is so. By *concentrating your full attention on everything you do at every moment* of your life you will obtain the same results as if you passed successfully through the whole course of the above-mentioned mental manual.

Why then was it written? would be a reasonable question. Because such concentration is too difficult and hard to practise for beginners, and not too easy even for advanced persons. The Masters alone are perfect in such concentration. That is the answer.

This concentration on one's own activities every minute of every day, which is necessarily connected with inner detachment from action—that is, merely the observing with the utmost attention, concentration in other words, the work performed—can be recommended to everyone who is able to do so. I used to do the same, since I performed what I wrote in that book. If you wish to know the secret of such an exercise and why it is so effective, realize that in it the consciousness remains untroubled and in peace while the mind's machine works apart from it.

When I am writing all that you are reading now, my mind is restricted to putting the ideas into words and sentences. There is no deliberation, or thoughts like: 'What will I write or tell now?', 'How should I frame this or another problem?', and so on.

Ideas come gradually and quietly from the Silence of consciousness, despite the fact that around me people may be speaking, apparatus may be working in a laboratory and sometimes there may be the need to observe its movements, and watch complicated dials, and so on.

I am quoting this practical example in order to elucidate for you, the problem concerning the role which the outer world may and should play in our lives. And that we have to be stronger than this world. Not by an 'exhibited' pompous display of strength which will be only proof of the opposite, but by a quiet, incessant stream of force in our consciousness, full awareness of what is going on inside and outside of us. This is the right attitude related to the title of this chapter. This book as well as *Concentration* has been chiefly written not in the peaceful silence of the study in my home, but just in the turmoil of worldly life, in the midst of other work. So no one should believe that it is conditions which prevent him from a successful study of concentration or even the paths leading to the Superconsciousness—Samadhi. The Maharshi answered the questions about the obstacles to inner work and progress, which apparently come from the worldly environment, when he said: 'It is your wandering mind and perverted ways of life which prevent your enlightenment.'

This enlightenment requires the solution of the great problem: 'The world and I'. You may find it by attentively following the material expounded in this chapter, thereby finding what relation should exist between your I and the world. The Maharshi taught that there is no such thing as active and conscious interference from the side of the world towards ourselves. The world has no separate I, will, or qualities in itself. It is just as we are, its components (I am referring here to the material manifestation composed of three planes, which we call 'the world'). Dominating and controlling our own three-plane microcosm we become able to influence the macrocosm.

On higher degrees, of course, it is possible only for exceptionally powerful and spiritualized beings. Then we speak about 'miracles', the foundation of a new religion, or the opening of new spiritual paths by Messiahs or other Messengers from Above—the realm of Truth.

Nevertheless, on a minor scale, everyone of us is contributing something to the world, impressing a good or bad influence on our surroundings, depending upon our own inner contents.

'A good man out of a good treasure bringeth forth good things: and an evil man out of an evil treasure bringeth forth evil things.' (Matt., 12, 35.)

In any case, we are responsible for everything which we bring into our environment. The world will co-operate with us and make our work easier, if we begin to apply the three 'commandments' of the Lord Buddha, quoted in the previous chapter. But the world will apparently be our enemy if we add burdens to its karma by our own foolishness and egoism.

Everyone should choose his own way, knowing of the reward for this which awaits him in the future. The law of cause and effect cannot be fooled, dimmed or avoided. How strange the primitive 'philosophy' of men seems to be, who, while recognizing the necessity of the law of cause and effect in the material world, would deny it in the more subtle manifestations of being! They know that energy does not disappear in the vast universe, but is only transformed into different forms. So why should the energy hidden in all our activities contradict this law?

Fortunately, it does not. The world and ourselves are co-related and bound together, until we set ourselves free from all relativity in the world of unique reality—the eternal illimitable Samadhi.

Chapter XI

Inner Strength in Us

Verse 448: 'By the knowledge that I (the Logos) am Brahman, the Karma acquired in a thousand millions of kalpas is extinguished, as is the Karma of dream life on awaking.'

Verse 508: 'I am neither the doer nor the instigator; I am neither the enjoyer nor the promoter of enjoyment, I neither see nor cause others to see; but I am that atman who is self-illumined and unlike (anything else).'

EFFORT is necessary to obtain a higher spiritual status by those who were not born with it, and surely no reasonable person would deny this. Similarly, Samadhi cannot be reached easily and without a considerable display of strength. Therefore, to our arsenal of abilities, we have to add the force which may allow us to overcome the numerous obstacles and difficulties on the Path, about which we will hear more in Part III of this book.

What is inner strength in man? Speaking generally it is a property of character which allows us to hold firmly to the chosen line in life, to remove and conquer opposing forces and so to reach the final aim. But there are several manifestations of that power, and to them this chapter will be dedicated.

(A) Inner strength is necessary initially for making a definite decision. Before we enter on the Path there are certainly many different ways which have to be considered. Some of them can be superficially more attractive and promise immediate gains in life. It is a well-known circumstance in occultism, that the strongest temptations assail a man just at the moment when he tries to leave the by-paths of materialistic and illusory strivings and desires. You can readily realize the futility of using your incarnations for temporary perishable aims, which leave you helpless at the end. You may well know about that terrible 'fire', called *frustration*, which tortures people who waste their lives. This suffering is bitter enough for an incarnate man, but it becomes really hellish when a man passes away from the earthly life to a new form, that of *results*. Then, no longer having a physical body, he cannot correct the faults and errors which he committed on the physical plane and which he now perceives so clearly.

And all this can still be insufficient in order to turn us to the right way, if we do not possess the requisite quantity of inner strength and firmness. There is no better method for developing it than the practice of concentration.

(B) When a decision has been made, and we try to take our first steps on the new Path leading to the acquiring of the wider awareness found in the Superconsciousness, new hindrances appear. These are distractions which arise, together with the *tendency to forget* what we decided to do every day on our new path. Then we have to fight them off, using our inner strength for the purpose.

Different people need different methods to do this and these are often too individual to be mentioned here as being suitable for the majority of us.

But the fulcrum of all of them will be an auto-suggested meditation:

'I *have decided about what I have to do to reach a higher status in my consciousness by raising it to Samadhi. I am entitled to realize it. It is my firm decision to do so. It is supremely good for me and nothing better could be chosen by me. I know that all obstacles sent against my effort come from the enemy. But my strength is greater than all temptations and I will reach my aim.*'

This is the gist of the self-assertion which is connected with this display of force. It can be used *ad libitum* as needed.

(C) More inner strength is needed for continuous effort. Later we will see that special meditations have to be performed regularly (Part III) and without interruption by any outer happenings.

This again requires certain force in order to fight successfully any disruptions in our specially established pattern of everyday life. We can no longer permit that, say, toothache cancels our daily programme and makes us retreat instead of going ahead. If we do not show our superiority over petty obstacles, how will we be able to withstand greater difficulties, which may (and usually will) be encountered when we are fairly advanced on the Path? This steady stream of power will be sustained in you, if you will persistently try *not to forget* where your true 'fatherland' lies, and 'who' you are.

By this we understand, the firm conviction that we are not the perishable body, and it is not at all our dearest possession, or even our fullest manifestation in this period of our experience, which still has a shell round the immortal core in it.

*   *   *   *

Years ago, when visiting the famous catacombs under Paris, with their millions of skeletons arranged along the underground streets and corners of that realm of death, I noted a very realistic sentence inscribed above the main entrances and avenues: *'We have been what you are now, but you will be what we are.'*

All is sad and silent in that abode of death, where only two colours exist, the white of the bones and the black of the inscriptions on the white shields on the walls. In spite of that, I noticed that many visitors to the catacombs seemed to be little affected by the ominous truth, staring at them from the high walls and niches. They walked between the walls of skulls and bones, betraying curiosity rather than insight into the silent speech of the human remains.

Something common to all weaklings is the avoidance of thinking about unpleasant things, especially death. In the second half of the twentieth century this problem of death is dealt with more often, and discussions about those who are dying are more frequently heard. But some fifty years ago it was different, and talk of death was rather shunned and held in contempt. Strength in man does not retreat before the thought of death, nor is it afraid of it. But we should discriminate between the fearlessness which comes from such strength and the hysterical bravery of a fool.

Samadhi is not a refuge for cowards, weaklings or ignorant people. Whoever of these three types tries to reach it must be prepared for bitter disappointment, for he will never be successful, and only frustrated to the end.

The origin of the true strength in man can be traced to the conditions in which this quality was developed and upon which it depends. *Firstly*, there must be an *element of knowledge*, which comes from experience. One knows *why* he should avoid any fear and weakness, when he remembers the painful consequences coming from surrender to these two vices. He should equally remember the positive results obtained by their suppression.

This is the normal way of evolution. But there are also people who possess the same knowledge without reference to the memory of former experiences. In such rare cases we speak about intuitional wisdom. This comes from man's distant past, that is from early incarnations, in which he developed these qualities empirically.

Secondly, inner strength should have as one of its roots, a philosophically developed conviction of its righteousness. A simile may be taken from the physical world: a more powerful and muscular man can perform more than a debilitated one. An occultist, knowing the old Hermetic maxim: 'As above so below, and as below so above', will have no doubts about the good reasons for being strong.

Thirdly, the development of inner strength is necessary for *fighting physical, emotional and mental* temptations, which are insurmountable obstacles to the spiritual consciousness in us. Here there cannot be any treachery. Man must be able to discard (even temporarily, if his Samadhi is of the Kevala type) everything that is relative and perishable in himself, before he can enter into the *Silent Temple*. Nothing else will do. Therefore we have to give closer inspection to the way in which to fight the three kinds of weakness-temptations in us. The way to Samadhi is not compatible with the crude practices of fakirs and other jugglers, who try to subdue their bodies by lying on nails, holding up a hand until it is withered and dead, and so on. Such self-mutilation does not give any real strength of character and will. For then a person can still be greedy (and usually is) for money, angry, and impatient in other realms of life, and so on. The examples of doubtful occultists, who trick naïve people, are sufficient support for this statement.

The inner strength in man should be manifested on the *physical* plane as an ability to be satisfied with very simple food and drink, used in reasonable amounts: not too little (as this will bring only starvation and a weakening of the physical machine, thereby sapping its endurance), but also not too much (indulgence in overeating breaks will-power and makes a man indolent). The voice of the body which requests some special foods in tasty varieties, and refined dishes, must definitely be suppressed. Here also belong the different habits, very common to contemporary men, such as the smoking of tobacco, opium, hashish, marijuana, and so on, which are definitely killers of will-power in man. The explanation is simple: everyone capable of logical reasoning, will accept that these habits are harmful, and yet, he cannot stop what is harmful for him, as dictated by his mind if allowed to think according to strict logic. The question then arises, and quite naturally: who is the ruler of such a man? Answer this problem for yourself, and it will be of great value to you.

Strength in relation to physical temptations and conditions is not any nonsensical self-torturing (which is, and can be only one-sided and therefore always insufficient), but just the *ability* to withstand all temptations at will, at any time and under all conditions. Deep psychology must be used in this matter, and in a very intelligent way. For example, you are very thirsty, which means that your body lost more liquid than it received. A glass of water will be sufficient to quench the real need—thirst; but you might feel desire for an icy cold beer, lemonade or other kind of drink. What will you finally do? The desire must be suppressed, the 'luxury' refused, and ordinary water taken instead of tasty substitutes.

In other conditions, when you have no special desire for a drink, friends may offer you a pleasant, cooling one. This time you can accept it without fear of weakening your will, for then your body is not trying to impose its desire on you. This rule will work well in almost all conditions of life, and it will not allow you to be overcome by 'foreign powers'. But there is another physical obstacle which is much more difficult to conquer—the sexual urge. It is not easy! No! It is very hard to be able to use our general rule of strength in this instance, for here activity and desire seem to be inseparable. This applies to everyone, with only an infinitesimal number of exceptions, and then only with truly exceptional men. But—you want to reach Samadhi, which will make you a most exceptional human being!

It would be useless to try to explain the special kind of psychology which operates in such rare cases, so the general rule for us will be: since you cannot serve both God and Mammon, you have to abandon one or another. Briefly, Superconsciousness and sexuality are opposite poles and in practice they can never meet. However, 'solace' may be given at this point: when you actually reach Samadhi, all lower desires will be eradicated and become void in a natural and most efficient way. But before this happens, efforts and inner trials cannot be discarded. As always, I am speaking about the *true* Samadhi, and not any kind of visions or other cheaper ecstasies.

*   *   *   *

Another source of strength is inner peace. Whoever has made peace in himself thereby possesses power. I am not taking into consideration the flashes of energy often met with in certain people, which may appear to be manifestations of inner force in them. True strength is quite a different quality. It is always available to its lucky possessor, who never makes any undue exhibition of it. After watching a mountain streamlet cascading down from on high, with much noise and splashing, and then observing the majestic flow of a great river like the Amazon or Mississippi, you come to understand the difference.

Samadhi, indescribable in any language of the mind, has as its forerunner this quiet, effortless strength in man.

Strength also means the absence of any fear. What is fear? The absence of self-assertion in most critical moments, lack of self-knowledge, and the presence of uncertainty, anticipation of future suffering, and identification of oneself with the body, plus ignorance of one's destiny and aim in life.

On such foundations is built the ominous castle of fear. The lowest manifestation of fear is physical cowardice in the face of suffering, which can damage or even destroy the visible body. A keen student will say, that all these unholy things have one source: identification (conscious or unconscious) with the physical body, and he will be right. Every evil can be traced to the body. In the name of, and for the sake of it all sins are committed, but never for the sake of the non-materialistic attitude. It is a vicious and tragic circle, this identification with the body, that fleshy cage, in which people suffer like trapped birds, throwing themselves against the impenetrable walls —until death. And the solution is so simple: it is fully realized in *Samadhi*, but it is anticipated, bringing immediate solace and victory over the nightmare of death, even *beforehand*, when man is advancing up the steps of the invisible, but quite real ladder, leading to the destruction of the tragic myth—'I am the body'.

Those who have read the first two books of my Mystical Trilogy (*In Days of Great Peace* and *Concentration*, being the first and the second respectively) and this, the third and last, will know the saying of the Sage Maharshi, who attributes all attainment to the final and wholesale destruction of the 'Body am I' idea.

The inner power in us does not destroy only wrong conceptions, otherwise it would be a street without exit. In reality, when we remove untruth from ourselves, the hidden roots of truth in us begin to send up their first tiny shoots, just like a germinating seed pushing its green stem into the air so that it becomes real and visible. It is exactly the same with the destruction of the falsity of the 'Body am I'. Then man begins to feel and perceive the growing proofs in himself, showing him gradually how he can live without identifying himself with his physical shell, and to live a much better, more reasonable, uplifted and imperishable existence. Nobody will give you any degrees until you pass all your examinations so as to show that you have performed some inner work, qualifying you for those degrees.

This is exactly the case with spiritual 'graduation'. We cannot and will not get anything for nothing. But, unfortunately, the mass of humanity believes in this nonsense. That is why, in our time, there are so many occult rogues, who try to exploit this foolishness in men, promising the latter that they will perform their work for them (of course, for a suitable reward) and 'initiate' them without any essential effort from their side. That is why so many useless books and 'teachings' appear at present, sometimes even meeting with a certain 'success' in their sales. But a few earnest and truthful books which do not conceal the truth of the necessity for hard work for any attainment, are less favoured in this twentieth century.

But it was the wise Romans, who knew about this, and said that: 'The world likes to be deceived.'

So many people prefer deceitful, but flattering words rather than the quiet and unpretentious speech of Truth.

To resume, we will end this chapter with a final comment: *Inner strength in man is one more condition for the attainment of Samadhi, the latter being just the realization of that strength developed into infinity.*

In Western Scriptures we find a statement, in which we are told that 'Heaven must be conquered by storm'. This fits in perfectly with our ideas about attainment of the Superconsciousness.

To think that one is weak and therefore unable to perform the necessary toil and effort is to commit temporary suicide, for it cuts away every possibility for such a man, and is lack of faith in man's highest principle—the invincible Spirit. The breath of death freezes a man who neglects in himself this germ of the Spirit, which aims at eternal Life. The Master of the West told us in His Gospels, when speaking of the relationship between the three manifestations of the One, that is: God the Father, the Son and Holy Ghost, that:

' . . . Every sin and blasphemy shall be forgiven men, but the blasphemy of the Spirit shall not be forgiven.

'And whosoever shall speak a word against the Son of man, it shall be forgiven him: but he that shall speak against the Holy Ghost, it shall not be forgiven him neither in this world, nor in the world to come.'

Perhaps, after having read the foregoing paragraphs, the great, mysterious words of Christ will become more understandable for us.

Chapter XII

The Great Law of Sacrifice

Verse 472: 'The great ascetics, who have abandoned desires and discarded enjoyments, who have subdued their minds and senses, knowing the supreme truth, attain at last *paranirvana* through union with the atman (the Logos).'

THIS Law also belongs to the corner-stones of Samadhi developing in us. What *is* sacrifice? Strictly speaking, it is the yielding of something attractive but of a lower kind, for the acquirement of a higher, although not immediately perceivable thing. That is why, outwardly, this sort of 'exchange' looks as if it is connected with suffering and—perhaps—with loss. Of course, these are only seeming disadvantages. An occultist developing will-power in himself would refuse to satisfy certain of his desires, thereby acquiring inner force and stability in his consciousness.

Admittedly, it might sometimes be awkward to deny oneself certain pleasures, formerly neither controlled nor sacrificed. But if a man knows about the benefits which can be derived from such a proceeding, he will always go ahead with it and so grow stronger and stronger.

Nevertheless, the first step may be devoid of the helpful knowledge, that the seed of sacrifice brings a rich harvest. Then he follows only the dimmed voice of his still infant intuition, but this makes no difference to the final results.

Now, what do we have to sacrifice, if we are to reach the aim—Samadhi? A technical answer would seem to be briefest and easiest. As Samadhi is the opening of the *absolute* (that is, spiritual) and universal consciousness in man, everything in us which is *relative* and temporal must be removed as being obstacles on the Path to Achievement. Such is the axiom presenting the truth, which is so much easier to formulate than to realize.

Therefore, we will dedicate this chapter to different aspects of sacrifice and the reasons for their performance.

(A) *Sacrifice in the Physical World*
Our body is our vehicle, but not our lord, as it seems to be to the

majority of men in this period. What are our duties towards that vehicle? The fact that we are actually in possession of it proves that we still need it, for the sake of the process of evolution. So we should treat it reasonably, in the same way as a jockey handles his horse. We have to feed it, according to its real needs. but not allow ourselves to succumb to the desires of this fleshly cage, and to indulge in luxury, excessive comfort, and so on. That this is the right way will be proved by the evident benefits which follow on from all reasonable training of the body. If the latter seems to be spoilt by our former indulgences, a process of purification may be indicated and then started, such as pranayamas (see *Concentration*, Part III), some kind of dieting and exercises. All this will be successful if our intelligence is strong enough to draw the right conclusions. For example, some people will say: 'Well, I can limit many excesses in my physical life, but I cannot stop smoking. It would make my life too dull.'

Let us analyse the problem.

An intelligently guided mind must accept that, say, smoking is a disadvantage for both our body and our will-power. Therefore, logically, this habit must clearly be abandoned, sacrificed. If you follow this decision, you have won a very important battle. If not, investigate what the obstacle is which is contributing to your defeat, and you will find that it is a physical desire for certain reactions in your body, produced by the use of the nicotine in your cigarettes. That is what the body likes!

Now, to whom do you yield if you cannot curb that desire? The answer lies with you. Not being able to take the first firm step, all the next ones become void. Then abandon your idea of raising your state of consciousness to the Himalayan peaks of Samadhi. It simply will not work. This is only one small example, but it may suffice, for all other conditions of the physical plane will be only variations of the one just quoted. Lack of the necessary degree of control over the body will strangle your efforts to concentrate, meditate and finally, to separate your consciousness from the cage of your brain. But there is a warning!

Fight only those physical obstacles, and sacrifice only the comforts which really bar your way. This *does not mean all the habits* on which your whole physical life is built, in so far as they do not actively hinder your efforts. If you prefer to sleep in one position rather than in another; if you prefer rice to potatoes in your diet; or black tea to white after your meals, and so on, it does not matter. It is not essential; but only for as far as you feel yourself fully capable of changing these habits at will. This means, that if you start to eat rice instead of potatoes and this makes little difference to you, you can please your body in this small matter.

But if the change of some habit seems to make you unhappy and creates inner trouble in you, *then fight it* until full annihilation is achieved. Otherwise, you will not be in a position to make any further advancement. I trust that I have explained the ways of physical control sufficiently in order to pass on to the next steps, the practising of the law of sacrifice in the emotional realm.

(B) *Sacrifice in the Astral*

This is a more subtle matter, as it involves the clear awareness, which in your life belongs to this plane. Enough has been said in Chapters III and IV about the *theoretical discrimination* between the astral and mental worlds, and we have to realize that the *practical application* will again be based on the performance of at least *two series* of exercises as given in *Concentration*, Part III. So there is no reason to quote from that book, as whole pages from it would be involved.

Therefore, an enumeration of the extent of emotional life which should be controlled and sacrificed, will be sufficient for our purpose at this point. The main principle is always the same: by sacrificing the minor emotions and desires we acquire inner force which leads us to far greater gains. Another principle equally important for the flight into Samadhi, but less known, is that unconquered and satisfied astral factors are like barbells bound to the feet of a swimmer. He must sink, as he cannot hope to hold his head above the surface. If duly investigated, the cause of this becomes clear and logical. You know that Samadhi means *freedom, absolute freedom*, from emotions, thoughts and all duality. If one of these three lower factors slips into your consciousness when you try to transfer it into the *Fourth State* (another term for Samadhi), the main condition just mentioned (that is, freedom) is not fulfilled and there cannot be any positive result, only frustration.

There is a very interesting fact: only the lower, disorderly or indifferent astral vibrations (that is, feelings and emotions) are obstacles in the beginning, and only this kind must be sacrificed. This refers to those specified in Chapter VIII which deals with negative astral. But positive, or as we usually like to say 'good' vibrations (love, harmony, inner peace, selfless attitude, and so on) are not obstacles, for they have no inquisitive or obtrusive characteristics. In other words, they do not become unwanted intruders when we need an absolute vacuum and freedom from all the influences belonging to the three material worlds.

Those which affect you adversely are defined as negative. Especially pernicious is that of *useless curiosity* which does not allow us to concentrate on what we really want. This obstacle has been extensively dealt with in Parts I and II of *Concentration*. The main thing about this particular obstacle is that at the time when you decide to perform some exercises or meditation, plenty of apparently urgent problems, all demanding immediate solution, arise in your consciousness. They do not attack you so strongly and persistently at times when you are occupied with plain, worldly everyday things. These kinds of feelings should be pitilessly rejected as they can easily frustrate your efforts.

More advanced students, who operate with mantras and theurgic techniques (short concentrated prayers and formulas repeated incessantly), may be attacked in another, more dangerous way, which definitely comes from some outer, inimical centres of force, and not from any good ones. This occurs when you mentally repeat an elevated sentence or prayer, and then, instead of a pious or wise word, *something* tries to insert a senseless, and often repulsive or even indecent expression. This happens when we are not sufficiently watchful and allow ourselves to repeat sentences simply by verbalizing them automatically, and not saturating them with the light of our consciousness, that is, not placing enough attention on their meaning.

Those who are affected by this obstacle say that it seems as if a 'foreign power' from the surrounding astromental space wants to spoil the inner work of the occultist. The best means against this type of intruder would be the putting of more attention on the mantras or prayers. Astral armour (see *Concentration*, Part III) can also be used. Those acquainted with the Western Tradition (Hermetism) and practical magic, may use their magic sword in order to dispel the turbulent astral currents condensing around them (see *The Tarot . . .*, Chapters III and V).

There still remains a recapitulation of all that has so far been said in this chapter, and the details described can be summarized to give us the following attitude :

> 'I am resigning and sacrificing all the astral world for the attainment of my aim, because only in that aim can I find the fulfilment of the Ultimate Truth in me.'

(C) Sacrifice in the Mental
At the present time we have much more to sacrifice from the activities of our minds than people did in earlier ages. Our minds are much more complicated, and we have developed innumerable categories of thought absolutely unknown to our early ancestors. This, of course, primarily refers to science, techniques, and everything connected with

them. But, this sort of mental development is of no use for gaining the superior kind of consciousness, as is Samadhi. Rather it makes it much harder for a contemporary 'civilized' man to achieve real control over his mental body, than for an Indian aspirant of Yoga, or even, for occultists hundreds or thousands of years ago.

The multiplicity of thoughts, terms, and complicated combinations in one's brain must be reduced, in the course of the training aimed at Samadhi, to only the necessary numbers, and finally, all of them must be eliminated when the target comes into sight.

We can summarize this by again repeating the chief characteristic of the Superconsciousness: in it *nothing relative* remains, only the *Absolute*.

What does it mean, that *Absolute*? That which exists remains, persists, when all that changes and all temporary attributes cease to be. If we apply this to our present mental states, we will see that actually there is little that we can 'take' with us into the great travel into the unconditioned realm of eternal Reality. Some people can even feel awe before the immensity of things which have to be abandoned. Some examples which should be carried out by the individual are:

Delight in never-ending reading, as well as interest in the mental creations of other men who are ignorant of the Path. This is because *nothing from the 'outside' mental ocean* can help you, but will certainly make your aim unattainable if you do not separate from it in good time.

Practically, it does not mean that every printed, written or pronounced word must be a *taboo* for you. At first glance a successful seeker does not differ much from an average man. He may well read his newspaper when convenient and may chat with his neighbour or friend, but if you could perceive the inner side of things, you would see that all these activities are only dreamlike, without any true participation by such a 'doer'. He is simply *not interested* in them, having concentrated himself on quite a different level. This is the right attitude.

Discussions and attempts to convert others to one's own credo also have to be sacrificed, together with all intolerance towards opinions, even the most ignorant, heard by us, for such behaviour would be as unreasonable as useless.

The stamina necessary for an earnest attempt to reach the higher state of consciousness is never born from doubts or painful convictions. Successful aspirants are rather *born* than made in their lifetime. Such people, from their earliest years, betray some deeper insight into their inner world, and imponderabilia, being more interested in these matters than the average man is with outer things.

If a decisive step has to be taken in the present incarnation of such a seeker, he will, in due time, encounter a book or a man who will give him the necessary hint and inspiration for the Path. But if the apparent interest for higher things arises as a result of the mental influence of a brilliant speaker or logical conviction, it will usually not be very durable and ought to be forgotten. That is why it would be quite useless to try to engage unsuitable people in a spiritual search.

Christ divided people into two categories, one ripe, and the other unripe. Even the Great Teacher had to recognize the fact of our different positions in evolution—as has already been quoted in Chapter IX—when He spoke about the dead burying their dead, and so on.

The student will do well to meditate about the impossibility of any wholesale equality in man's evolution. Always there are highly developed individualities, who have succeeded in rejecting more veils from their shells, and who, therefore, see more and better things around and inside themselves. If perhaps, religions are more suitable for 'mass consumption', the hard path of Samadhi is seldom trodden, and the chance of encountering and the privilege of knowing a fellow-traveller is very slight.

Some fifty years ago (I am writing this in 1960), the subject about which we now speak quite freely in this book was unknown except to a very few occultists, both in the East and West alike, and relevant literature of any value did not exist. I am referring to the great idea of attainment of the high state of consciousness called *realization of the Self in Samadhi.*

But a spiritual giant came in the person of the Great Rishi Ramana, and now everywhere you may find his ideas discussed and even followed. From time to time highly evolved souls give a push to those who are ripe enough, and are able to catch the opportunity and engage themselves on the Path, one of the first steps of which is multilateral sacrifice of former, dear illusions and mental bypaths. The term 'sacrifice' is being used not without forethought, for our mistakes, wrong ways of life and errings are possible, not because we actually hate them, but strangely enough because we love them. So the process of getting rid of them is rather like that of sacrifice, until the full Light begins to radiate on us at the end of the thorny Path.

Another kind of mental activity which must be cancelled is the nursing in our minds of fantasies and their derivatives, such as *false hopes*, expectations, dry verbalizing, and efforts to perform the impossible: to initiate the mind into the mysteries of spiritual reality, which is not a result of mental development. The latter, of course, goes parallel to spiritual growth, just as the face of a wise man has an intelligent expression, but not the reverse, for that face does not

86

create a sage. As Frenchmen say: 'when snails appear in the garden, we know that rain is coming, but it does not rain because of the snails.'

Here are some inspiring lines from the well-known occultist—A. Horn:

'There is no sacrifice, because one who gives the best he possesses will be given something much higher and better than he had.

So, where is the sacrifice?

He who gives of his love will live in Love, and all the sorrows of separation will leave in their place the *joy of the union*, because what one gives, that will one gain.

The joys of Heaven will be given to him who renounces the joys of the heart.

There is no sacrifice, because he who breaks the attachments of the heart, breaks the bonds of his soul.

Getting rid of everything is to enrich oneself of *That* which is higher than everything.

Everything will be given to him who possesses the spirit of sacrifice, but everything will be taken away from him who does not possess this spirit.

And truly I say unto you, that he who will lose his life will find it, because he will enter into *That* which is the Eternal Life.

So, there is *no* sacrifice.'

The following quotations about the idea of sacrifice come from another of my books—*The Tarot, a Contemporary Course of the Quintessence of Hermetic Occultism*, Chapter XII:

'The power of *sacrifice* is *supreme*. It is among those men who sacrificed the *most* for their minor brethren, that arise the real rulers and transformers of our planetary lives. The greater the sacrifice, the greater is the authority and influence of the being, who has mastered the real form of spiritual realization and illumination. There was a *Man*, who wanted only good and only light. And He was subjected to every form of human suffering.

'His closest friends and disciples left Him alone in His most difficult and tragic hours, when He was anticipating His torture and death. One of them even betrayed Him into the hands of His reckless executioners. . .

'He accepted all in the *spirit of sacrifice* which lived in Him. And the result? This *Man* now rules over the most essential elements of life on this planet, the same which so cruelly repudiated Him almost two thousand years ago. . . .

'Sometimes a man, listening to the words which come from the realm of the *active spirit*, as is the case with the *fulfilment of sacri-*

fice, feels his heart caught in an inner movement, as if in an earth-quake. From that moment onwards he is lost to the *relative and temporal*, but gains the eternal and absolute.

'Through the supreme initiation of the *Law of sacrifice* all Wisdom is also attained. Who has sacrificed everything knows everything without effort and toil. Who has sacrificed everything has conquered *Life*, unlimited in time and space because he has sacrificed all that is relative, over which rules the phantom of death. . . .'

*   *   *   *

The Cross as the 'symbol of sacrifice has a unique power of realization when applied with faith and a pure heart. You may get proof of this in your everyday life. When you think deeply about the *sublimeness of sacrifice*, that is, when you meditate about it in your heart's sanctuary, the world and men around you become changed and then you are able to *see* this fact, not only imagine it.'

*   *   *   *

So, with these excerpts from *The Tarot*, we will end this chapter.

Chapter XIII

The Law of Transformation

Verse 491: 'I am not the doer, nor am I the enjoyer, I am
without change and without action. I am pure intelligence,
one, and eternal bliss.'

IF in our present state and period we cannot enjoy Samadhi, it means
that changes in us are necessary; in other words, transformations
must occur, which finally make us able to transcend all of them,
reaching the eternal, unchangeable state, which is final. In former
chapters we termed this process 'rejection of the veils', as in reality it
is. But because of that it does not cease to belong to the category of
activities defined as 'transformation'. This word is especially good, as
if even etymologically it is concerned with 'forms'. And it is only the
forms which change, not the inner *Core*—the *Self*, which is unalter-
able. We can, and should accept it as logical, but still theoretical
knowledge. If we cannot yet attain the Superconsciousness, it is
because we still need many transformations. They are undoubtedly
an *immutable law* in the *realm of forms*, being the clothes which
enwrap the immaterial contents.

All manifestations of life undergo incessant transformations, from
stones to mammals with man at the top. For example, the substance
of a rock is crushed by thermic and atmospheric influences; later it is
washed down a stream to become fertile soil. Plants use it for the
building of their stalks and foliage. The latter may be eaten by
animals or humans, becoming components of their blood and bodies,
which serve as forms enveloping the invisible principle the Consciousness. In these paragraphs we are speaking about physical transformations, astral and mental ones will come later.

The law of even physical transformation affects every human
being. We can accept as truth, that the more developed consciousness
—*Self*, clothes itself in finer material forms. Here I do not mean any
conventional beauty of bodies, which does not always coincide with
the degree of inner evolution of a man, but simply the quality and
development of that physical matter in the body, which apparently is
the subtlest one and stands just on the border between two different

worlds. It is the brain and also the nerves. Both are less fine and susceptible in primitive men.

As an example, let us take for granted the fact, that primitive races generally have a much less developed surface (that is, convolutions) to their brains and less sensitive skins because of greater distance between the ganglions. Several years ago I read about some scientific experiments which were conducted in the matter. Whereas a white-skinned individual will feel two different pin-pricks on the skin of his back distant by, say, two millimetres, it will be about twice the distance for a negro. From this we can see that there are essential differences in living forms, and the same in psychology and mentality, which is too well known to be mentioned in detail.

Otherwise, it means that astral and mental conductors are also different in different kinds of human beings. So there is not, and cannot be any equality from the scientific point of view. But there is a much more important factor common to all men : the immortal spiritual *core*, which we already discussed in former chapters and which has only one quality—*perfection*.

It is like the pure sky : below there may be rain, clouds and destructive storms, but we know that *above* all these phenomena there is the cloudless, stainless, unspoiled by anything, eternally free blue sky. We see this when the clouds are absent.

And it is because of this factor that occultists insist on the general brotherhood of all men. Still more advanced beings do not distinguish between any form of life, as they are able to *see* it behind each form. That is why the Maharshi understood the animals around him and they were able to understand him; why St Francis of Assisi preached to birds and was not afraid to go into the forests, where hungry wolves ranged in winter, attacking all other men except him, and why Albert Schweitzer will not allow an earth-worm to dry to death on a sunny path in his garden, but will remove it and put it back in the protective humidity of grass.

In this life we have our forms (as bodies) and we are to a certain extent limited by and dependent upon them. We cannot deny this fact, even if we profess that we know the unreality of matter and the sole reality of the Spirit-*Self*. This does not refer to the exceptionally advanced beings, like great Teachers of humanity, who dominated their sheaths to a degree unimaginable for us; but eventually the law of transformation had to be fulfilled, and their bodies returned to the general reservoir of matter, which fact we call, decomposition after physical death.

All this has been mentioned in order to clarify the action of transformation in matter. Our bodies are different to those which we possessed in our childhood, in size, components, development and quality of the organs, and also in the ability to respond to different kinds of vibrations in consciousness. These bodies become different with advancing years, until they are unable to exist as separate complicated organisms, that is, then they die.

But here again there is no equality. When the average human being advances in years he becomes less active, and astral and mental functions also lose their former vigour and alertness, while senility and even idiocy may occur. But more developed people do not lose their intelligence and activeness, and just the opposite happens. They remain brilliant and wise to the end of their lives, even advancing in these qualities with the passing years. Inner development evidently overrules the influence of age in such men. Innumerable examples are known and can be found in the biographies of great men, and the curious student will himself find what he wants as proof of these statements. So many scientists, composers, statesmen, and so on (also saints) have not and do not succumb to old age and have displayed alertness of mind and energy until death. We can find enormous comfort in this for we see that the 'contents' prevail over the outer shell. Developed consciousness transforms their bodies according to their needs and aims.

On this plane the vibrations of the Self are reflected as consciousness, that active intelligence operating through the brain, which is the finest physical matter on this planet, as is sometimes confirmed by science. But extremely fine vibrations, connected with the manifestation of highly evolved life, need an accordingly developed brain. This cannot happen with a baby or child and this is the cause why, say, Christ and the Maharshi reached full expression of their greatness only in early manhood, when childhood and adolescence were over.

On our own way to the Superconsciousness we have to undergo similar transformations. Special exercises and sometimes ways of life are aimed at this. Now it may be clear, why, for example, in a reasonable course of concentration the exercises must be extremely carefully formed and placed, so that a gradual and harmonious development and transformation in man—not only in his astral and mental, but also the physical plane—can take place, in a secured evolutionary and not a dangerous way.

In the emotional realm (astral) the law of transformation works similarly to that in the physical world. The intensity, clarity and range of our feelings from the cradle to the grave underlie the constant changes. This is understandable. But for our purpose, they should be transformed in a definite and calculated pattern, which you have read more about in the foregoing chapters. In order to approach

Samadhi, our emotions must be controlled, put into the desired order and then selected, that is, which of them have to be discarded as useless or harmful, and which retained until the final discarding of all astral, dissolved in the ocean of Superconsciousness, which does not need any of them.

This effort, concurrent with a course of concentration, leads to the transformation of the astral body. Instead of a formless 'cloud' round the physical silhouette, it becomes more shapely, and the colours in it become arranged harmoniously, gaining in clarity and purity, as our training advances.

But there is no need to be clairvoyant, and to *see* this process for ourselves. The thing will be done, and the property of our emotional life will show itself, no matter whether we can see it directly, or only perceive the change by the *results*. Becoming quiet, self-confident, not irascible, balanced, fearless, well intentioned for everything and everyone, devoted to a spiritual ideal, all this will prove that we are duly advancing towards our target. For no man with a disorderly astral can ever dream and hope to reach Samadhi. The Highest cannot be cheated! Those who have reached this state know about it experimentally, but novitiates should know it first in theory (that is why all this has been written) in order to avoid mistakes born from ignorance. Such is our method.

The section of the training which will be given in Part III can be summarized in the already quoted *third* commandment of the Lord Buddha: *purify your own heart*. Christ said the same in other words: *'Blessed are the pure in heart: for they shall see God.'*

It seems that no further explanation is needed: *transform your impurity into purity*, that is all.

The last application of the law of transformation will be in relation to the mental realm in us. After what you now know about the two previous planes (physical and astral) you are certainly in a position to foresee how the process of transformation works in our minds when we are on the Path. By performing a course of concentration we gain control of the thinking process. It seems to be simple, but it is not so. Once the physical and astral are naturally controlled by your mind, you have to find the master who will be able to rule the mind itself. *Who is he?* On this level I would not like to burden you with classical terminology, both used and misused. All this will be only verbalizing, that is, indulgence in the way of thinking forbidden to those who are on the Path or try to enter on it (see Part I of this book).

Therefore I say: *you alone are entitled to control your mind*. It is not a paradox. Look deeper into that sentence and then see what it was intended to express. This statement indicates that you are necessarily above and beyond your mind, as was the case with the emotional and physical worlds. As the real *You*, the *Self*, cannot have any name (who could treat the Highest as an *object* and label It?), it is up to you to reach *It*.

The fact, for example, that the Maharshi reached the ultimate Samadhi (Sahaja Nirvikalpa) does not grant the same attainment to all those who gathered at his feet.

Everyone has to work for himself, just as everyone has to take his own food and digest it in order to live. This simile is based on the old but true Hermetic axiom : 'as above so below.' But there should be no mistake : no one should seek, according to these rules (belonging to his mind), the *Self* as something separate, *apart from himself*. This is the *destructive blunder*, most often encountered, which leads only to nonsense and useless erring. The consciousness of the true I will grow and gradually arise as the conquest of your mind goes ahead (see Parts III and IV of *Concentration*).

The true *Self* will not be discovered, but it will *transform* you utterly into that *Self*. Still, in another way, it will tear off 'the veils' from round the Core. Of course, there is also the famous Vichara (see *In Days of Great Peace*) but it too is only a means, an excellent one, but *not* the aim itself. The Maharshi in his incompatible concise-ness and exactness of expression and definition told us that the 'Vichara is like the stick which is used to light a funeral pyre. It too will be consumed together with all the fuel and the body.' Here the dead body means the lower, the false self, that is, the ego-personality, which has no real existence, being like a deceptive mirage.

This very enlightening fragment of the Sage Ramana's teachings can be extremely helpful for the seeker who accepts it.

After the process of the transformation of your mind has success-fully led to the achievement of full control over it, two ways lie open before you. Only *one* of them leads to Samadhi, as we will see later. On the first way, a man may become a powerful yogi, an occultist or magician. If achievement has set the successful adept on the *right* side of things (the white Path), the three titles will be almost synony-mous; but if he engages himself on the *left* Path (the black) his name for the particular incarnation will be that of—*black* magician, who holds to the wrong (or 'shadowy') side.

Both kinds of men (although for different purposes) will strengthen the currents of thought created or followed by themselves, in order to achieve realization of their aims. One may try to help his less developed brethren by creating a new religious system or philo-sophy, an Egregor, and so on, supporting the evolutionary triangle, as Hermetists would say.

The other will act quite differently: he will try to create involutionary currents, pulling men down still deeper into materialism to seek new pleasures of the flesh and ambition, of sensuality, attracting people of the descending (involutionary, that is evil for us at the present time) triangle.

But the way of a Samadhi seeker will be very different. He will use his newly won power of transformation for his actual aim, that is, the reaching of the absolute *freedom* from all incarnations and material life, which is Samadhi. It will probably be only of the 'Kevala' type (temporary, sporadic) in this life, but Kevala, as the Maharshi said, will, and must be transformed into the Sahaja (perennial) and then: '*The dewdrop slips into the shining sea!*' for ever. It is Nirvana, Salvation or Liberation, according to the founders of three great religions: Buddhism, Christianity and Vedanta.

To speculate about that state is useless, as none of us has even experienced it, so nobody can speak of it. That the subject is impossible to be communicated in words or thoughts, is clear from the many sayings of the spiritual Teachers, who knew the *subject* and *State*. But we are *not* comparable to them, even when we reach the Kevala, the reflection.

The Lord Buddha said that we should not try to fathom what is unfathomable, nor try to measure what is immeasurable, for he who asks errs and he who answers errs, so we should not speak at all. Christ stated: 'Eye has not seen and ear has not heard the bliss which is prepared for the righteous.' And the Maharshi said: 'For which purpose is all this talk about the Ultimate State (Natural State or Sahaja Samadhi)? Talking does not lead to any solution. Realize the *Self* and then all questions will be answered by themselves for ever.'

It is an interesting fact, that those who are fairly advanced on the Path are the least curious of people. They never ask to try to get any mental (that is, in words) explanations referring to their ultimate aim—Samadhi. Of course, it is possible that a period of hard training (based on concentration and domination of the mind) burns out the vice of mental restlessness, and with it, its daughter—curiosity. But personally, I think that here the cause may also be due to that mysterious attachment to the *inner peace*, which, once experienced, gives full certainty, unruffled tranquillity and balance in us.

It is this latter quality of which we will learn more from the next chapter, which ends Part II of this book, in which we have been occupied with the problem forming the threshold and first steps on the Path to Samadhi.

Chapter XIV

The Law of Balance in Consciousness

Verse 154: 'A wise man must acquire the discrimination of spirit and not-spirit; as only by realizing the self which is absolute being, consciousness and bliss, he himself becomes bliss.'

THE last of the main approaches to Samadhi is the acquiring of balance in consciousness. This term has various meanings in relation to the subject of this work, and so we will consider it from several points of view. The central idea of inner balance seems to be simple. No astral or mental storms are allowed to disturb the aspirant, if he does not want to delay his achievement very considerably. This point is also common to the rules for all occultists, who have aims different from Samadhi.

From this we may conclude that this balance is essential, and we will be right. As usual, we will analyse the emotional realm first. If we cannot hold our astral in balance, it means that emotions dare to arise in us spontaneously, uncontrolled and unchecked. Instead of inner peace as a necessary forerunner to Superconsciousness, we will have a life full of emotional storms, no matter what their origin. From the technical point of view, *passionate love or hatred,* for example, equally prevent the dawn of Samadhi in us. They can provoke certain kinds of ecstasies, it is true, but from Chapter VII we know what relation ecstasy has to the true Superconsciousness, devoid of all visions and storms. It is an obstacle, and as such it will always be avoided by the wise aspirant.

For building up a more clear conception of inner balance we will use a simple example, which gives us an outline of the very idea of perfect balance in us. Imagine a rod, hanging by a cord attached to it just in the centre. Then it will take a position parallel to the floor, or horizontal. We then say that the rod is in a well-balanced state. We can, however, apply a slight push to the rod, and its end will swing up and down for some time. These movements are symbols of our astral disturbances and storms. If the rod represents our state of astral consciousness (it may also serve us as a symbol in the mental world), then we will see, that there are many points on the rod which produce different amplitude of swing, depending upon their distances from the centre. These points will change their formerly ideal horizontal positions, which they had when the rod was fully balanced.

The closer to the centre, the shorter is the amplitude of swing, and vice versa. But the centre itself remains immovable. It does not swing at all, despite the fact that the whole object is in movement. Therein lies the solution of the enigma.

In order to avoid swinging (astral vibrations) we have to place ourselves just in the centre. Then still being on the astral level (which cannot be avoided if we are still not free from the necessity to incarnate), *we do not participate* in its vortexes. Hermetists, famous for their exact thinking and practical philosophic attitude, offer this symbol which I have used here for a different purpose. Actually, they do not take just a single rod, but two of them to form a square cross and seek the central point which keeps the figure in a balanced position, like our rod. This *cross* then, with its perpendicular shoulders, represents two worlds: astral and mental, contacting between themselves, but still entirely different.

This conception may serve us well in our attempt to visualize the working of inner balance in us: *to be a witness of all our surroundings, which belong to the arms of the cross; but at the same time, to be immovable and not participate in any of the swinging.* This is the wisdom of true behaviour for us.

Meditating about this idea, the student will come to the required attitude and then, to its conception, which will be alive in his consciousness for ever. This will assist him at the time, when he will feel the swinging of his life's cross to be dangerous for his inner balance. The Sage Maharshi explains the same truth with his usual supreme simplicity when he states how we should obtain our emotional and mental balance: 'Be a witness, *not* a participant of all that happens around you in all conditions. Do *not* be attached to these conditions, but just free from all attachment.'

If we do not possess some required quality we should duly undertake training, in order to develop it. In this case a simple exercise will help us to create that detachment. The exercise has different phases according to the planes on which it is performed. We begin from the lowest, that is from the physical one. Learn to separate yourself from your bodily frame. In many ways this will bring you incalculable boons, including peace in the hour of your departure.

Supposing that you have already performed some special exercises as in Series I and II of *Concentration*, this then, should not be a hard task for you. Take a walk in a quiet garden, or on the paths of a park where there are not many people about. Try to transfer your I (Consciousness) beyond your body, which means that you imagine that you see your body from above (distant by some three to four feet) and from behind, about seven feet away. Observe as if you were just this distance apart from your walking form. Watch the back of the head, shoulders, torso, but all the time mentally insist on being *apart* from them. Exercise in this way until you are quite successful for a short time, say for a minute or two.

Next, try a little longer, but three minutes will be quite sufficient. But you may also, in very propitious conditions (when no one is in view or expected), measure the limits of your performance, that is, attempt the exercise for as long as you can. This will give you more self-confidence, which is essential for all inner work.

Later, perform this 'separation' in some more complicated ways, when travelling in a train or walking in a street full of people, *but never when driving a vehicle yourself.* There are highly developed occultists who can do even this without any danger to themselves or others, but it is not essential for your present purpose. The point should be made, that you are *not* abandoning your physical counterpart, but are only withholding your direct presence in the body, while still exercising full 'remote control' over it, and not allowing it to do anything without your will. This is different from the true 'separation' which occurs with the exteriorization of the astrosome, practised by advanced Hermetists (see my *Tarot*) and having aims other than those given here.

Generally, this exercise of 'walking behind one's body' is not dangerous if performed exactly as instructed, except in a few rare cases, where such temporary and controlled separation may lead to an abandonment of the body, resulting in its collapsing into a kind of lethargy or catalepsy. You yourself may see where the danger lies. Such people cannot practise this exercise outside their own rooms. This happens to those who have mediumistic inclinations, being rather animistic than intellectual in type, and not endowed with sufficient will-power. Therefore, this path is too hard for them.

When practising this 'separation' from your body, you will find many positive privileges obtained as an additional and unexpected reward. When you have to perform physical work, connected with considerable strain, the 'separation' from the body, as mentioned before, will give you much more stamina and ability for far greater efforts, and the periods of tiredness will be considerably reduced.

All this can be successfully done only with movements which are well known to you and which you are accustomed to perform without any mental strain in your everyday life. That is why the first example was only ordinary walking. You cannot (and should not) attempt to separate from the body when working at something which needs perliminary deliberations, and thinking on how it should be done.

Several cases are known to me, where people have used this method when working at their routine tasks. Results were produced with much less strain, and with more speed and efficiency. Our body is a strange instrument, not wholly known to us. It seems to possess its own counterparts of a man's astral and mental worlds. This has been scientifically shown in the tables of human elements in the ancient Kabbalah. Interested students can find it fully covered in my *Tarot*, Chapter X. This hidden and dimmed consciousness having rather an automatic character, connected with the performance of certain movements, can be observed in skilled musicians. Take for example a violinist, who transfers the melody written down in notes, directly into movements of his fingers, working without any attention from the side of the mind. This means that the artist does not think where he should place his fingers when taking every necessary note from the score. In other words, the notes (and their inherent melody) are automatically transformed into movements of certain parts of the performer's body, which press the strings and move the bow.

But it is very hard to do this exercise of 'separation' in conjunction with uncommon physical activities, such as handling a mechanism with which we are not yet familiar. Anyway, this is not required for our purposes.

Spiritually perfect men (Masters) seem to use their physical bodies exclusively in this 'separated' way, which is normal for them. When I saw the Maharshi, the first impression was just that : this man uses his body as a remotely-controlled machine, his true I being virtually absent from it. He was so different from his environment, from all those Brahmins, Europeans and other kinds of men round him, in the large dining hall of his Ashram. Of course, this was only a fragment of his achievement, rather an insignificant one, a slight reflection of the inner beauty and power of a man, who has attained the Highest.

When the ability of 'separation' (as just explained) is acquired, there comes the next degree of achievement of balance in the emotional realm, or, as we used to say—in the astral. The method is the same : *until you separate something from yourself, you cannot master it*, that is, control all the movements as well as their cessation. As everywhere, a certain degree of the power of concentration is essential for success. If you cannot silence—even for a short time (a few minutes)—your emotional vibrations, when you want to (the same with thoughts), how can you observe them, being, as you are, absorbed and mixed up with them?

The general pattern of the necessary exercises, similarly as it was with the control of physical walking is to sit relaxed in the asana (as given in *Concentration*) in a quiet place or room; evoke some simple feeling, like the remembrance of the pleasure you experienced when stroking the silky fur of your pet cat, of listening to a well-loved melody, and so on. Do not be disappointed with the apparent simplicity of the first steps. You will probably find quite enough difficulties when trying to perform them as required and intended.

Without this simple beginning there will not be a successful conclusion, so the writer wants to give you something which will really allow you to stand finally on your own feet and become independent of elementary instructions. Scriptures treating of Samadhi can give you only texts, valuable, of course, but *only then when you are able to use them*. Innumerable thousands have read these texts, the Upanishads, Vedas, works of Patanjali and Sankaracharya, and the teachings of the modern Master—Sri Maharshi, but how many of them attained the very aim of all this uplifting literature? A great Christian ascetic and spiritual philosopher, Thomas à Kempis, who *experienced what he wrote, and did not merely concoct it from his mind or compile it from the words of others*, wisely says: 'Every Scripture must be read in the spirit in which it was written.' The meaning of this is none other than without suitable preparation one cannot expect any profit from even the most sublime exposition of truth. The chapters of this book are written just in order to help an earnest and conscientious seeker to form in himself a suitable approach to the Consciousness of the Future, as the mysterious Samadhi can be termed. For *no one*, the greatest Teachers included, can *give* to an unripe person what he cannot realize, understand and therefore, strive for. *This should be firmly understood when reading these chapters*. Men are liable to expect some thundering words from Teachers, which will immediately transform them, and turn them into angels, despite the fact, that they are still full of relativity in their lower desires and egoistic ways of life. This can never happen.

One beautiful summer morning, eleven years ago, when I was sitting at the feet of my Master, a gentleman entered the hall in which the Maharshi lived, sitting on his couch and giving his Darshan (or personal appearance) as the Hindus say.

The man was a leading engineer from a large Western firm, which, I believe, delivered locomotives and other machinery to Madras. Hearing about the powers of Bhagavan (an honoured name for Rishis, with a meaning close to 'divine')—as well as being slightly acquainted with the so-called 'Self-Realization' movement in the U.S.A., founded by one of the minor Indian yogis—he bluntly, but with due reverence and sincerity, asked the Master Maharshi to give him Self-Realization before the evening if possible, as he had very important business in Madras and had to return there, leaving the Ashram before sunset.

Do not let us be like this otherwise quite decent man, but who was deeply merged in basic ignorance of the character, techniques and true aims of a spiritual search and attainment.

When you have succeeded in evoking some emotional vibrations in your consciousness according to your own choice and will, dismiss every one of them with the firm: '*Go away!*' Then try to remain free from all emotions for a while. This will be successful when you can kill all interest in them, as was directed in *Concentration*. A helpful technique would be, if, simultaneously with this exercise, you also use the techniques from the first one of the physical degree, that is, separation from your seated body, just at you did before walking, and so on. Then say to yourself: 'I see the fact that this Mr X or Mrs Y is now experiencing this feeling.' By certain practice and endurance (which is a key to success) you will gradually reach what you need. The emotions created and observed may vary, of course, according to your own choice. But do not use any complicated ones, especially at the beginning and not for too long. Two or three minutes for clear observation will be quite sufficient in each case.

The next step—perhaps more difficult, but absolutely attainable—is the same 'impartial observation' of your feelings, induced, not artificially by yourself, but by your everyday life. Someone says something to you, which provokes certain movements in your astral. Do not identify yourself with them, but *observe* them. What you will discover by practising this method is hard to predict exactly, as individual experiences and ways differ in details. So we will not enumerate them here, only underlining the most essential points.

You will realize your *separateness* from your feelings and from that time forward you will be a changed person. Then full balance and harmony in your astral will become an accomplished fact, and again this will push you a step closer to the Samadhi for which you are seeking. It now remains to control and balance your mind. We need a brief and simple definition of this element in our consciousness. Elaborate theories and complicated, empty terms will not do. Therefore, why not borrow the knowledge from those who really *know*? As the Master Sri Maharshi once told his attendants: '*Mind is only the thoughts, the sum total of them in you.*'

If you accept this axiom, all inner work will be greatly helped and made easier and faster.

The basic method for obtaining a balanced mind is similar to that which before was applied to the astral. The average man's mind is like a boat without a helm tossed about on a choppy sea. Such a man does not know from where his thoughts come or whether they are really useful to him for his purposes. There is an excellent and unbeatable method for absolute domination of the mind. It is the *finding of its source*. How can it be done? Unfortunately, very little can be added by speech to these words, that is, the *seeking of the source*. This must be performed in the state of passive concentration, when all thoughts are, for a while at least, expelled from the mind. Then create *in yourself the will to enter into the farthest recesses of your consciousness, where thoughts arise, the beginning of the mind*. This should be done without words, with only the pure abstruse effort to reach the aim. Finally, in order to complete this necessarily scanty definition, it may be added that the process of '*seeking' the source* may be visualized (or symbolized) as if you are applying the diamond-sharp drill of your inquiring consciousness to an imaginary channel, making it deeper and deeper. But such comparisons are often dangerous, as sometimes students try *to materialize* them, and to think about such non-existent *drills* as if they were real. Therefore, to conclude, it may be added that under no circumstances can a word be mentally used in the above-mentioned process of seeking the source, for all verbalizing must be utterly destroyed, as a habit which bars the way before you.

As a result of a successful attempt, one enters into the awareness of the supermental consciousness, from which he can then firmly establish harmony in his mind, as required for Samadhi. I expressly said 'the awareness of the supermental consciousness', *not the consciousness itself*, which is at the end of the Path, when almost all troubles have been eliminated and all exercises successfully performed.

Another method is similar to the astral research previously mentioned. From the state of inner concentration (passive) watch your passing thoughts like clouds in the blue sky. Observe this process *from apart*, belonging to Mr X or Mrs Y (your name), but *not* to that, which you feel to be the real *you* in the moments of such interesting and otherwise unusual psychological experiments. These are less difficult than they appear to be at first glance. They are quite possible. Endurance, as everywhere, will be the measure of your success.

I do not wish to say that everyone, without exception will be able to perform such a search and thereby establish the full balance as required in his mental counterpart. If, while reading this and trying to catch something with this simple exercise, you feel absolute darkness like an impenetrable wall before you, it might well be a sign that the whole endeavour is premature.

Now, let us take a brief look at the actual meaning of that inner balance in us, achieved in order to obtain a right approach to Samadhi.

(1) *Physically*, you will no longer be subjected to all the whimsies of your body, its nerves, moods and desires. You will be able to still it whenever you want to, thereby reducing its resistance to the minimum. Know that an unsubdued body is definitely inimical to your higher aims. And so it is with your astral and mental. There is neither place nor purpose here to investigate *the cause* of such a state of things, as it does not belong to the subject. But this problem, important for purely occult studies, is widely covered in Hermetic Philosophy (see my *Tarot*).

(2) *Astrally*, you will not be thrown from one emotion to another, giving you no breathing space for the establishment of peace in yourself. For, experimentally you will know the nothingness of astral storms in relation to the higher life and aims.

(3) In the *mental* plane you will be in a position to find the necessary starting point, which leads to the inner silence, the silent mind, being the antechamber to Samadhi. Those who have reached this state know of its importance for every spiritual search. We can find this term, inner silence, sometimes hidden under different technical or mystical expressions, depending upon the category of men using it, as with many Christian Saints, Hindu mystics, genuine yogis and Rishis, Sufis, the ancient and true Rosicrucians, eminent Kabbahlists and Hermetists. If the exponents belong to the Western Schools of occultism, they will often depart from the very term 'Silence' using symbols and similies, borrowed or adapted from Alchemy, as did Paracelsus, Martinez de Pasqualis, Marquis S. de Guaita, and sometimes Eliphas Lévi.

*   *   *   *

Only one thing matters: *to find this Silence, and not merely talk about It*. Unfortunately, rare are those who find and numerous are those who talk, without having had due experience.

PART III
En Route

Chapter XV

Inner and Outer Obstacles to Achievement

Verse 151: 'As the water in the tank covered by a collection of moss does not show itself, so the *atman* enveloped by the five sheaths, produced by its own power and beginning with the *annamaya*, does not manifest itself.'

THE third part of this work is reserved for the exposition of an active method, which may lead a successful and enduring aspirant to his aim. If in Parts I and II we were occupied with conditions and passive preparations, here we try to step on to the actual Path to Samadhi. *The student should never forget that he cannot take these steps until he has fulfilled the conditions indicated in former chapters.* He cannot be a 'green beginner' in Part III of this course. He should possess a considerable degree of concentration, as a basic and indispensable quality of his mind. He should also have a certain moral standard as mentioned in the chapters of Part II. From numerous letters which reach me from my readers and students of *Concentration*, I can see where difficulties lie for them in relation to the realization of the instructions given in that book. And so this must also apply to the present manual. Then why not anticipate these doubts and questions?

Well, the first trouble with the majority of readers will be that they may immediately try to perform what they find in this Part, which is a sort of 'way' to their aim. There will be small hope for them if they are not ready with the conditions as shown at the beginning of this chapter. The main weapon for the attainment of Samadhi is right and persistent *meditation*. Meditation is the higher function of the highest *material* principle in man, which we call the *mind*.

I deliberately say 'material', for these three human manifestations, which we call *physical, astral* and *mental* are conglomerates of matter, and great analogies exist between these three. Just as you cannot expect an untrained, sickly, or simply weak physical body to perform any outstanding sporting feat, so without suitable preparation of our subtle (that is, astral and mental) bodies we cannot hope to be outstanding performers in their particular realms. We will never get right meditation of itself unless we are saints or genuine yogis, which terms mean men who have performed all the preparatory work in their former incarnations and now are merely reaping the harvest.

Meditation is a normal, natural, higher function of our mental counterpart—or body (see *In Days of Great Peace* and *Concentration*, where many chapters have been devoted to the problem of meditation). So training is necessary, and I presume that you agree with me, even from a purely logical point of view, and will follow the next seven chapters with full attention and make practical use of the material contained therein. This is the best guarantee of success. The task is undoubtedly hard, as was the case with *Concentration*, perhaps the hardest that a human being can undertake. But, if you feel a real urge to climb to the peaks, covered with the eternal, virgin snows of the absolute, pure Consciousness (which after all, you are even now), this means that a *mysterious call* has come to you from those heights. This *call* is unerring. It does not come to those who are not in a position to begin to perform the ascent. That is what every student should know, it is his *first real initiation* into the Truth of Being. It is perfectly possible to spend lives, one after another, without hearing this *call*, as happens to the large majority, to the millions. If you wish to follow such a path, which begins in the ignorance of birth and ends in the uncertainty, unconsciousness and suffering of death, it is entirely your own business. One cannot be other than he is.

As has been stated, this part of the book will develop the theme of meditations. A set will be used, which was given without commentary at the end of *Concentration*, as a final touch for the successful student. Now we have to make full use of these seventeen verses, which lead to Samadhi, giving an outline of the mental activities and attitudes useful for starting true meditation. The latter, as we already know from Part IV of *Concentration*, is beyond all mental processes of assessing the theme of meditation in one's mind. This is all we can do. For that which ends the mental effort and begins the new world for us (the 'Fourth State' see *Concentration*) is beyond the language of the mind, and therefore cannot be expressed in words, or given through the medium of any book or conversation. But a good start may mean a good result.

Verse 1: *I am not what this world calls* me, *my name, body, feelings and thoughts, because in a comparatively short time all these will cease to exist.*

The first part of this sentence is—according to the classical rules of occultism—a *negative* one. Why is this so? Simply because we are absolutely unable to define what we really are. This is expressed in the

famous Advaitic formula mantra : 'Neti! Neti!' (Not this ! Not this !).
We can only deny that we are not any of the perishable things.
What remains is our true I. There can be only *one* sole thing, and
we cannot say that everyone possesses It, for the truth is, that It
possesses every one of us (as we still believe ourselves to be separate
beings). Stop now and think deeply about this conception, until it
becomes a clear truth for you. The rule of meditation is, that we cannot proceed with any further development of it if the preceding parts
are not devoid of all doubts for us. Otherwise there will be only loss
of time that will lead to disappointment. The laws ruling the higher
mental activity of man (that is, meditation) should, and must be
observed. Some occultists call the highest point of meditation—where
there are no thoughts at all—*contemplation*. We disagree with this
definition, as it is inexact and not scientific. *Contemplation* requires
an object, and when meditation generates the thoughtless state, it
goes beyond subject and object. So why use a term which does not
have a practical meaning for those who really meditate, instead of
merely speaking about it, without having experienced any higher
state of consciousness? Let us be strict and brief from the beginning.

Returning to Verse 1, we see that all labels with which the world
provides us, must be rejected. Actually your name is meaningless. If
you wish you can change it for another label, as equally devoid of any
real meaning as was the first one.

In former chapters we had to learn *not to confuse* ourselves with
not only our physical body, but also with the two subtle ones. This
cage of flesh is certainly mortal and devoid of all reality of existence.
Go to a cemetery and look at the graves of your parents or grand-
parents. Where are their bodies which you knew so well when they
were 'alive'? They do not exist any more. The same will happen to
you, and some living consciousness, clad in a still living shell (body)
might come to your grave and go through the same thoughts as you
have done.

Meditate about this chain of events in order to set yourself free
from the deadly, all spoiling and destructive illusion '*I am the body*'.
It is a heresy ! As a result, the last trace of this lie must be eradicated
from your consciousness. Of course, at first you will realize this only
as an intellectual conception, but later, it will become a living, inner
truth in you. It is an interesting law : to the measure that you rid
yourself of that wrong idea by the way of *negation*, a *positive* assertion of that which you are, apart from your body, will grow in you,
substituting the former subconscious belief.

So there is no fear if you follow our Path. Now comes our divorce
from feelings and thoughts, from our astral and mental shells. If

separation from the physical body was successful, the getting rid of the astral and mental will not bring many difficulties. We will proceed further.

'I am not my feelings, for they come and go. I can even create them (for example, by means of the power of my memory, and so on), destroy, exchange and forget them. And I can be free from all emotions when I concentrate on the inner Silence in me. Therefore, there is no doubt that the astral is also only a shell, but never my *I*.' Now meditate.

* * * *

It will be similar with thoughts. The same proof as we had with feelings confirms for us, that our consciousness (our *I*) can well exist, and be aware of this existence when we disconnect ourselves from the mental ties. The same concentration proves the existence of our *Self* beyond both thinking and thoughts.

In Silence we still exist, although there is no object nor subject. Now try to create the kind of inner stillness you learned from *Concentration*. And then say to yourself: 'Now I have experienced the truth of this meditation. I have no doubts any more.' Meditate on this theme.

Verse 1 has the purpose of destroying your inner obstacles in all three worlds. With outer ones there can be difficulty, and the methods of fighting them must be different. Generally speaking, the first and chief hindrance is our own karma, and that of those closest to us. We have, despite all appearances, to accept the truth that destiny always puts us in the best possible ways and conditions from the evolutionary point of view. We can think differently, but this will be just another burden for us. We should *do our best* under all circumstances, and this will suffice for every karma. Not everyone can be a millionaire or some other kind of potentate, but also, not everyone must have bad health, unpleasant conditions of life, and so on.

Always remember the famous tale about the man who complained about his heavy 'cross' in this life (that is, karma, as we call it) and was allowed by God to choose a new one from among the millions shown to him, which belonged to other people. He tried them all, and finally found one which seemed to be the most comfortable for him. He asked the Lord to give him that cross. Receiving it, and placing it on his shoulders, the man realized that it was his own old cross.

Nevertheless, we are quite entitled to try our best in order to improve our outer conditions, if it is possible. I would like to add: entitled only at this time, at the beginning of our Path; for to the measure of our inner progress and growing wisdom, the desire to change our conditions vanishes like the morning's mist under the sun's rays. For then we appreciate our 'inside' more than 'outside'. But for the present, we may encounter numerous obstacles to our enterprise such as: family conditions, a disturbing environment, apparent lack of suitable rooms (for meditation), lack of time, and so on. All of these can, and must be overcome if our will to step on the Path is strong and genuine enough. I knew of a man, who was greatly impeded in his inner work at home, because his wife and family were hostile to his intentions. He could not find a quiet room and relatives mocked at his 'yogi's practices'. Not wanting to destroy his family life he arranged to reach his office earlier than necessary, and so had some time for meditation. Also, after work, he visited the nearby church for half an hour, when it was usually empty at that time. Then he was able to perform his inner work without being disturbed. This is only one example, but there are many other solutions, suitable for each person.

Worse than outer obstacles are the inner ones. The chief ones were explained at the beginning of this chapter. What remains are the minor vices in our characters like: laziness, doubts where there is nothing to doubt, fear, inaccuracy, bad habits, and the great ruler of them all, the old enemy—*egoism*, in all its gross and subtle forms.

Without departing from truth we cannot give very exact means to fight each of them, which would be suitable for everyone on every occasion. If someone does, he deceives himself and others. Our method is the development of a power in us, which may then crush the obstacles (vices in this case) one after another, without making any distinctions between them.

And this is the force of our will. Think about just why so many men, who by no means seem to be ignorant or stupid, recognize their faulty behaviour, and even speak about the right ways of life. Yet, in spite of all this, they continue to lead their miserable or wrong lives, bringing suffering to themselves and those around them. Where is the true cause of it all? Evidently a mental conviction is insufficient. *Will-power* is the real factor which should carry through every decision. Some people are perfectly aware that, for example, smoking or drinking, and so on, are slowly killing them. They want to live, but they lack the will-power to cancel their bad habits. This power must be developed and then it will break the obstacles in and around you.

The general method is: *to learn to overcome impulses and desires.* This is the key. A similarity exists here with the athlete, working with his barbells and other equipment in order to develop the muscular power which allows him to perform feats impossible for untrained men. The principle here is the same: as muscles grow and gain in efficiency, they systematically overcome resistance (in this case weight), and so the fact of overpowering our desires develops strength in human will. This must be thought through with great attention, then realized and accepted by the earnest student on this Path. And there is no substitute for this method, because in occultism, as in ordinary life, it is hard, even impossible, to get something for nothing. If we can still cheat somewhat on the physical plane because of the gross matter which is its main component, it would be beyond all possibility on the two higher planes, on which there is no chance for earthly gambling. Here a weakling can disguise himself, but he will not be able to do the same 'there' where all things (feelings and thoughts) are instantly visible to the other inhabitants of the subtle worlds.

I gave many details about the development of will-power in my other books, but they are so important for this work, that I am compelled to repeat them here briefly.

First, choose your 'barbells', that is, the desires or habits which you have to 'lift' or remove, to suppress. Do not use anything useful or good, as it would be detrimental for you. There are plenty of undesirable habits on which you can perfectly sharpen the scimitar of will. Sit some day, having secured a couple of hours for this first battle, and make a check of your useful and useless habits. You may note them down on paper. Select those which common sense tells you need to be overcome, removed at the first turn. For example, do you smoke? If so, then know, that this weakness will bar your path to Samadhi if you continue to surrender to it. Here no compromise is possible. The thing is, that when you will have to make a greater effort, demanding considerable will-power, you will dissipate it together with the smoke-rings from your cigarettes. It is a strange psychological experience : when we really need our will to be a sharp and piercing force, our unsubdued negative (in other words evil) desires raise their hideous heads like desert jackals and bite through your weak decision. But every victory over them makes them weaker and you stronger. Always have this in mind when completing your 'list of proscriptions'. When it is ready, begin with the smallest item on it, otherwise you will fail. Many years ago I began with such an apparently insignificant habit as eradicating that of crossing my right leg over the left when comfortably seated in a chair. This advice I owed to an old occultist whom I knew in my youth. And it was not so easy as it may appear to many readers. In due course the 'big game' came later.

Learn to refuse to yield to your unsubstantial desires. Do you wish tonight to see a film which attracts you? Think : 'Is it necessary? Will it add much to the treasure of my knowledge or experience?'

Give the answer impartially to yourself and *then act accordingly*. Have you the desire to chat with someone on an indifferent theme? Place it before your inner tribunal for sentence ! Are you in a hurry to get home today? Make your way from the station or bus (or your car, and so on) longer by three to five minutes, by making a small detour. After each of such 'victories' say to yourself : 'I have done it. I have the power to do greater things, to do everything I wish.'

You like to have a cake after your meals? Then for some days delete these beloved titbits from your menu. But be reasonable and do not starve your body, for even true asceticism as observed by the spiritual giants has never been devoid of clear insight and knowledge of what the body can bear, and what it cannot. Beginners do not possess the mystery of domination of spirit over matter, which can achieve what we call 'miracles'. St John de Vianney, the celebrated 'Curé d'Ars' (1786—1859) was physically a weakling, and yet his main daily food in the second half of his life was mostly a cold potato and stale bread. He mortified his body to such an extent, that before he died, he asked that the usual funeral rites for priests be dispensed with, because he did not wish to scare anyone by the sight of his severely martyred body.

And yet he died at a fairly advanced age and nobody would accuse him of suicide. But the same hard life could easily ruin the health and perhaps bring an early death to a layman, who would dare to ape the Saint, while not possessing his iron will and mysterious spiritual support, which made his body resistant to all the mortifications which he inflicted on himself. Extremes are *not* necessary for our purpose here, and the contemporary respresentative of the highest spiritual attainment, the Great Rishi Ramana, did not practise any visible asceticism at all. He slept and ate just like those round him. But I doubt whether we can find in human history another similar example of such superhuman will-power as was his. He sat giving his Darshan (presence) almost to the end of one of the most excruciatingly painful sicknesses known to medical science, and for eighteen long months, renounced hospital treatment and the proper care, which would have taken him away from those who came to see him for the last time.

Normally, in such cases the patients are heavily drugged in hospital to prevent them becoming violent from pain.

For us, gradual progress is most essential. When the developing will-power brings many 'rewards', the student should decide the plan for his enterprise for himself. Will-power grows proportionally to the efforts made, that is, the greater the sacrifices and renunciations, the greater are the results and powers. Those who need to use exceptional forces put into play an enormous amount of self-restriction, thereby 'charging the battery' to the utmost.

In conclusion I will quote from Sankaracharya's *Viveka-Chudamani*, Verse No. 377:

'For one whose self is controlled, I see no better generator of happiness than dispassion . . .'

From this we may see, that by sacrificing lower things, we gain the bliss of the highest.

*   *   *   *

Here a warning must be given. Under no circumstances should the aspirant take on too many problems at the one time. This means that you should not attempt *at once* to eradicate, sacrifice or restrain too much. If you would like, as from today, to stop, for example, smoking, drinking, eating your sweets and cakes, crossing your legs, looking in every shop window on your way home and to detour three miles before you allow yourself to enter your home, all these things will certainly end in failure and you will actually perform nothing, merely tiring yourself and losing energy, which is necessary for every effort. Apart from that, you will simply forget what you should and should not do now. If at this stage you are beaten in even only one of your early decisions, it weakens your will instead of fortifying it, and the work must be done again from the beginning, with the additional burden of your shattered belief in yourself. This must be avoided for any price. The bulk of defeated aspirants belong to just those men who wanted to do everything at once, and who finished by performing nothing apart from becoming frustrated, which shuts off any further progress for them for long periods.

Therefore, we should be reasonable and firstly undertake an easier problem, to solve it successfully, and then to pass on to another, perhaps a more difficult one. In such a case you will be in a better position every time, and your self-confidence will operate and grow according to your successes.

When will-power is considerably strengthened in you and you can renounce more serious things successfully, then you may reach another stage, that of the actual use of collected power. Exact instruction together with all technical advice cannot be given openly, because there are mysterious moments which defy all description. Anyway, he who has succeeded in building such a power will know how to use it actively. Our purpose is to destroy the obstacles on the way to Samadhi. A powerful will can affect the karma of a man, and this is the right meaning of its use on the Path. The gist is that if a man, possessing the accumulated power of innumerable suppressed desires, really wants to perform a difficult task, all this power is at his disposal and can be thrown on to the scales. More cannot be told, but a simile may be enlightening. Take a small amount of explosive powder equivalent to that in a round of ammunition. If fired in the open it will not produce an exceptionally strong display of force, even if placed in a closed container; but collect the powder from a thousand such rounds and the explosion will be tremendous.

When a man, having innumerable conquered astro-mental elements (desires and strivings, plus thoughts) to his 'credit', *wants something,* this effort of his will has a great realizable power. When a spiritual Master, who has conquered *all* desires, weaknesses and attachments, uses his will for his lofty purposes, you can easily guess what the result will be. That is why, in some Eastern sacred books (Upanishads, Vedas), the 'perfect yogi' credited with absolute non-attachment (which means full conquest) is considered to possess the attribute of omnipotence. I hope that now the great idea of where lies the source of force in man is clear to you.

Saints and eminent occultists are known for their miraculous cures, resuscitations from death and other superhuman feats. But there is also another, much more mystical aspect of such things, leading to omnipotence. It seems to be simple in speech, but not so in attainment. The man who has reached absolute detachment from all illusion and everything relative has *no individual will any more.* He wants nothing for himself, no matter in which world he may manifest himself. Then his will necessarily becomes *One with the Omnipotent Will of the Whole* (you may call it God). This speaks for itself and no more explanation is needed.

This conception is the basis of why Hindus ascribe to their genuine Gurus (spiritual Masters or Supermen) all divine powers, and why they say: 'Who sees the Master (Jivanmukta in their terminology) sees the Lord Himself.' A Great Teacher once told us: *'I and the Father are One.'* 'Because I came down from heaven, not to do my own will, but the will of Him that sent me.' Such is the mystery of will and the power inherent in it.

*   *   *   *

There is a mental pit into which the aspirant should not allow himself to fall on this path to Samadhi. In the last dozen or so years, many books have appeared in English by Eastern authors, which have titles connected with classical Indian Yoga, in its *Hatha* aspect. But if you read them attentively, the only thing you can really find in them is an attempt to teach Westerners cumbersome physical contortions which enforce the body to do all kinds of gymnastics, almost impossible for a normal man to perfom, and to twist the body into hideous knots and unnatural postures. These things are recommended (along with numerous pictures of such performers) allegedly for the purpose of dominating one's body, and then the mind, and so on. But all this is really nothing more than a caricature and deformation beyond recognition of the fine Hatha Yoga, as is known from the classical Hindu Scriptures and in its Western exposition by Ramacharaka.

Authors of such books promise perfect health, almost unlimited youth and very long life to their followers. But if we look closer at these 'masters' we will invariably see that they themselves practise only until middle age while their bodies are still flexible.

They cannot stay the normal process of ageing, and ailments affect them just as much as they do ordinary men, perhaps even earlier. And as cures they do not use their own prescriptions very much, but seek conventional medicines and drugs. Yet there are still men who believe in such impostors.

True Hatha Yoga includes some physical exercises, as well as breath control, but in a reasonable and graceful way, as a useful addition to other higher Yogas, such as Raja, Bhakti or Jnani, because these may help the student to still his mind before meditation and so regulate his astral and mental functions for better balance.

However, the above-mentioned worthless substitutes and exaggerations can only help the 'master-authors' themselves, as a source of easy income from royalties and lessons.

Our body is merely an instrument, and it is unreasonable and frustrating to sacrifice one's life to its sole care, forgetting the most important thing, our spiritual aim. Moreover, the physical practices of Hatha Yoga, even in their pure form, as mentioned previously, are useful only while being applied, for when exercises stop for a few weeks, the benefactory influence invariably fades. This was one of the reasons why I abandoned this way many years ago. Let the student be warned by these lines and not allow himself to be led on bypaths which only augment the obstacles ahead of him.

Not every obstacle on the Path can be overcome, and not everyone can reach the consciousness of the Future—Samadhi, in his present life. Unripe people may be unable to perform the necessary inner work, about which we are speaking in this book.

There can also be karmic obstacles not to be overcome in this incarnation. But all toil in the right direction will never be lost or frustrated. Sri Aurobindo Ghose rightly expressed this idea when he said: 'The impossibility of performing something today is only a proof that it will be done tomorrow.'

Usually, people who are absolutely unable to approach the higher aspects of consciousness are *not even interested in it*. Such things are as if non-existent for them. On the other hand, keen attention in that direction—no matter whether negative or positive—might be a sign of certain possibilities in a man.

The Master Maharshi was once asked how it was possible that St Paul, who was an ardent foe of Christianity in the early period of his life, persecuting, torturing and even killing the followers of the new faith, later became one of the corner-stones of Christ's Church. The Sage replied that it was immaterial that St Paul formerly hated Christ. The important thing was, that in him was always the thought about Christ. We may accept this as confirmation of the value of faith, even if it differs from our conceptions in relation to the object of that faith. Faith is always an attribute of Life. What may be and is wrong, is its *absence*, together with indifference, laziness, stagnation and consequently—decay. These are only the attributes of death, not of Life.

Verse 2 : *But I am for ever.*

This is the next meditation used in our fight with obstacles on the Path. Being simple it does not need much explanation.

My *I-Self* cannot be annihilated. If it manifests now, even in these limitations of the incarnate life, certain tendencies towards the Infinite, the Eternal, it is proof that these germs are in my true I. Men can forget them but not lose them. So truly, I am for ever.

This pattern of meditation should be used until it becomes the normal attitude of our awareness of the imperishable life, which we really are.

Verse 3 : *I am the one who controls all these sheaths, I am above and beyond them.*

This meditation is a detailed assertion of one's essential being in relation to one's bodies. We are so engrossed in them, that we can never remember too much, nor be reminded often enough about our non-material I. If you meditate diligently, you will gradually come to the inner conviction of the true I in you, which so far, has remained undiscovered and unknown.

The transfer of our 'centre of gravity' in consciousness (this is not too explicit a term, but it is hard to find a better one) from the relative, material attachments to a spiritual conception is not an easy endeavour, nor a quick one. Eons have passed in the slavery of matter (Maya), so how can we expect to be suddenly able to reject the amassed beliefs, superstitions and attachments to sensuality and the five senses? Who promises such a thing is a deceiver, and a very harmful deceiver. Unfortunately, too many of them are swindling and feeding on naïve and ignorant people.

The aim of this verse (3) is to help you to establish yourself, *apart* from firstly, your visible and later, invisible shells. When this is achieved, things appear to be simple. From being the doer you become only an onlooker in the drama of your life, or like an actor, who really plays the role, without ceasing to be himself. *This is the whole truth told briefly.* And this is our aim at this stage. The onlooker, or actor, does not actually suffer what is presented in the theatrical drama. Many small technicalities can be used in order to accelerate this process of *separation*, but the majority of them are taught only orally by the teacher, being restricted from being made public, because they might appear to laymen and untrained persons as too strange and even cumbersome or weird. Nevertheless, they are often very efficient if duly understood. But there is a simple means which will bring the maximum benefit if practised. *Start to treat your personality, that is, the physical form, name, position, outer appearance and habits as a 'third person'.* Try to refer to it as 'Mr' or 'Mrs' and so on, as if *you* were apart and observing this gentleman or lady from a certain distance. It looks like a trick, but it works better than many other 'secret' methods. There is a prominent Indian yogi of today, who has adopted this method even in his official life, and always refers to himself in the third person, avoiding the use of the pronoun I. Quite a useful attitude which is also beneficial for the disciples of his ashram.

First of all you should start with your bodily appearance, and when you are ready you will see, that the *separation* and the becoming an observer of your feelings and thoughts instead of the doer, is much easier than it was in the beginning with your physical shell. This exercise should be steadily performed under all conditions, but gradually. Later it will become a constant source of inner joy to you.

Any approach to Samadhi is void until the experiences arising from this exercise are fully mastered. I think that another practical piece of advice would be useful for every earnest aspirant. When some astral influences are exercised on you in the course of your everyday life, that is, when from contacts with other people you receive some emotional impressions or shocks, you probably feel them in the area of your solar plexus, that is, between the end of the breastbone and diaphragm. This is because a very important nerve-centre is situated there, which, briefly speaking, is the link between the physical and astral bodies. That is why people usually say that all feelings are reflected 'in a man's heart'. Actually, it is not the area of the real, physical heart, which has little to do with astral communications, but just that of the *solar plexus*.

When trying to 'separate' from your physical counterpart, as just recommended, you will probably feel that the most difficult part was the stopping of the reflections of your feelings just in the centre below your chest. Therefore, one of your practical efforts should be directed to preventing your emotions from affecting the solar plexus. This can be done only by deep meditation about your undoubted independence of the physical body, and especially, in the point of contact of the *plexus*. *Leave* it and stay some six feet behind and above; this is the only advice which can be given in words. However, it is sufficient.

*   *   *   *

There are still more obstacles of a purely physical character, which come from the aspirant's own body. You cannot allow it to remain in a state of impurity or disobedience, if you strive high. An idea which has sometimes been expressed by certain occultists of not-so-great knowledge, is that : 'conditions of the body do not affect man's inner (spiritual) work.' Perhaps it is a very tempting conception, for it tries to disregard all care for the physical form, apart from feeding it and going to sleep. But this is impossible. To allow the body to remain completely unfit and impure means nothing else than the inability to control it, even in a most elementary way. If we are not ready with our lowest vehicle, how can we hope to dominate the astral and mental bodies which are more subtle and therefore more complicated in their handling? Lack of any control bars our way to the Path.

This is not to say that the aspirant must care about every possible 'perfection' of his body, making it completely healthy, athletically strong, and so on. It would be superfluous and unnecessary. But he should forbid himself any laziness and unhealthy way of living, all excesses and useless habits, as has already been mentioned in foregoing chapters.

A very weak and disobedient body will not allow you any considerable attainment in, say, meditation, for a brain provided with insufficient and unhealthy blood refuses to be a good conductor between the consciousness of the waking state and that of the true I. Until you reach the state of the supermental consciousness (while still incarnate), you will still be dependent upon and rely on its instrument, which is the brain. If you are able to transfer all your consciousness beyond the three lower planes (physical, astral and mental), then you will care little about anything else. But this happens only when one is very advanced and has victoriously passed through all lower states. As you can see, it is a circle and nobody can escape from it, or trick the Law of Evolution.

So we have to develop a certain plan for our physical life, in order to harmonize it with our inner strivings. Periods for regular sleep, for taking food, for work, all these should be reasonably established in advance, and the rules created and followed faithfully. Food has importance, for it affects the body's effectiveness, and wrong feeding results in difficulties in controlling the body. Heavy meals, meat, alcohol, tobacco, strong tea or coffee are undesirable from the same point of view. They adversely affect the capacity of the body and especially of the functioning of the brain, which then becomes slow and inexact. We know that no meditation is possible after the use of alcohol or narcotics. Swedenborg noted that heavy food was inimical to his spiritual flights. Moreover, his visions became gross and incoherent when he indulged in excess of food and drink. In his writings he mentions that one day, while merged in ecstasy, he got a *direct warning* and a '*voice*' said to him: '*Don't eat so much!*' He obeyed this to the end of his life (see: James—*The Varieties of Religious Experience*). Fresh air, walking, swimming, light garments where possible, moderate sunbathing, some physical exercises (if you are compelled to lead a sedentary life), are always indicated and recommended within the measure of karmic possibilities.

But any exaggeration in control and care of the body, any ascribing to it of a deciding role in inner advancement is as wrong as complete neglect of it. Therefore we are against any of the practices of the now so-called Hatha Yoga exercises, which only absorb all of a person's energy and do not leave enough for the much more important thing, concern about our true I (Atman). Cumbersome positions and contortions are only another proof that such a 'yogi' is essentially a deep materialist, and the foremost 'reality' for him consists only of visible and tangible things, with his own body presiding over them.

All this has disfigured the formerly pure ideas about Yoga, which term is now almost exclusively connected with the physical practices just mentioned. The more venerable, higher Yogas such as: *Bhakti, Raja and especially the Jnana,* have retreated into shadow for the majority of Western as well as Eastern seekers. Instead, there has appeared another anomaly, that of delving into the texts of the Hindu Scriptures. Unfortunately into valueless commentaries made by incompetent persons, and not into those which are most valuable and offer a real way to Attainment (like the works of Sri Sankaracharya and Maharshi, Ashtavakra Gita, Ribhu Gita, these being practical manuals, although given in a veiled form making them accessible only to more advanced seekers).

This can also be another hindrance on the Path to Samadhi.

The difference between knowledge and Wisdom in Samadhi is a

most interesting problem for many seekers, who still have not reached the superior state of consciousness, and who remain in the realm of mental cognition, whose formula is *'duality'*. This means that they have not yet solved the final binary: I and Non-I. Only those who possess Samadhi can speak about it in a satisfactory way. So I will quote the Maharshi. He told us that the Sage who lives in the realm of the unique spiritual reality (Samadhi) is both *ignorant* and *omniscient*. The *first*, because there is nothing in the manifested (temporary and therefore unreal) world, in which he is interested or wants to know. The *second*, because nothing remains for the Sage to know any more, which is equal to omniscience.

But there is another point. If a Sage is incarnate, all the powers of the mind are also at his disposal, although he is always reluctant to use them, just as we do not like to use horses and cabs for travelling, preferring the superior means of fast cars, planes, and so on. But when a Sage needs to give some teachings to the 'sons of mind' (as we usually are), he must then use the language of that mind—words.

Now, compare the sublime exactness, clarity and conciseness of the words of Christ or Maharshi, and you will understand that the possession of the superior state of consciousness also gives the best possible command of the lower states, among them, that of the mind. Wisdom in Samadhi is closely connected with man's freedom from thinking and feeling. This means that then he is *not compelled* to perform any of the aforementioned activities. These are great words for those who are able to understand them truly, or *to live them* in the consciousness. Our present state of ignorance is just that of compulsion. The majority of us cannot imagine existence without the visible world that surrounds us, and without thinking and feeling (that is, mental and astral impressions and activities). But the Superconsciousness—Samadhi—is just the *Pure Being*, the silent and all-embracing Wisdom, that light which does not allow any shadow.

All knowledge necessarily needs two opposite principles (1) the knower and (2) the known, which form a binary. To these is added a third element, the fact of knowing. All of this is in relativity, and therefore only temporary, not possessing the attribute of permanency, because there must be, and are, incessant changes in the relationships between these elements.

There is no place for Samadhi while such processes still exist in the consciousness: just as the disturbed surface of a pool will not give us a clear reflection of ourselves. We must wait until the waters are completely quiet.

Wisdom in Samadhi is the result of the cessation of movement in us, that is, of compulsory movement. Temporary manifested life depends upon movements and changes of all kinds. Eternal and absolute Life is Peace attained for ever.

Not many will be attracted by such a prospect, and this is the reason why Samadhi, in all its splendour, cannot be reached by the majority of human beings.

Chapter XVI

Defeats and Downfalls

Verse 166: 'Because the false conviction that the self is merely the body, is the seed producing pain in the form of birth and the rest, efforts must be made to abandon that idea; the attraction towards material existence will then cease to exist.'

THE most ardent desire and intention to enter the Path leading to the final rest for the human spirit, to Samadhi, is no guarantee of Attainment, as some cases prove. There are many factors which can put a brake on the most intense of strivings; but usually, men do not know about them or about their karmas, which can forbid them to reach the highest aim for several incarnations.

In this chapter I will try to explain the most common causes which may bring about the downfalls on the Path. Apart from those which will be mentioned presently, there can be other circumstances, purely individual and seldom encountered, which cannot be foreseen and included in general rules, and hence speculation about them will not be of any use to you.

The *bulk* of defeats belong to *lack of endurance* in the aspirant. It can be said that more than ninety per cent of unsuccessful attempts are caused by this fault. Therefore this point is worthy of your particular attention and analysis.

What actually is lack of endurance? The primary cause is, of course, weakness of will-power in a man. This creates the inability to hold steadily to intentions and realize them in one's life. Such a person will gladly recognize the salutary aims he wants to achieve and will understand their beneficial influence on himself, but, when the time comes to act according to his convictions, he does not confirm them by deeds. The effort necessary for realization of his lofty aims becomes an insupportable burden, and under its impact he gradually forgets, and later, renounces his strivings. Anyone who permits himself to be subdued by a habit, has weak will-power, which will make his endurance on the Path very questionable. Such people fall away like yellow leaves from a tree without achieving anything worth mentioning. Lack of will-power usually signifies lack of effort and self-discipline in one's past, extending back beyond one's present life. Other particulars about will-power and its role were spoken of in Chapter IX and others.

Endurance can also be affected by an insufficient inner conviction of the value and importance of the whole enterprise. Sometimes the downfall of the aspirant, who has successfully passed through the first stages of the Path (acquiring the ability of concentration and the beginnings of meditation), comes because of a sudden disappointment and loss of enthusiasm, and with this the necessary energy to pursue the Path. Many causes can be responsible for this kind of failure, the main ones being:

(1) The aspirant's mind was not sufficiently subdued and therefore not cleansed from the building of mental clichés based on pure fantasy. One may create false and unnecessary pictures of the future state of Samadhi. This is a serious error, deforming meditation and preventing purification of the higher mental state in man, which is the first condition for initial flashes of the Superconsciousness. The student then, after working for some time, sees that he *has not made any progress* and apparently consciousness has not received any enlightenment to justify his efforts. He allows his mind to wander on the bypaths of sterile thinking and doubts, instead of compelling it to regular meditation. Then the inner balance (see Chapter XIV) becomes lost and with it—the Path.

(2) If sensuality has not been utterly eradicated in the student, but only stunned by efforts of his will and by practice of some special occult training (use of mantrams, setrams, and Hatha Yoga exercises), it *may some day rise again* like a dog running away when his chain becomes rusty and breaks. In such a case the hostile forces will not omit to send him immediately one hard temptation after another. If the aspirant has not yet certain spiritual power and experience in himself, or has not secured the aid of a true Master (see *Concentration*, Chapter IX) he will undoubtedly succumb like the monk Paphnutius in Anatole France's *Thais*, and finally lose the Path, entering into the muddy stream of sensuality and all its illusions.

(3) If the power of concentration has been insufficiently developed, the student cannot cope with the assaults of thoughts during the time of his meditations. The deep root of this failure lies hidden in the fact, that in this case the disciple has not experienced the great peace of his true *Self*, and therefore has not been able to build a solid 'Inner Sanctuary', which was discussed in Chapter IX. This means that *he has no sure refuge* against outer influences

(in this case thoughts) and therefore cannot approach the peaks of Samadhi. This circumstance is frequently encountered in some unsuccessful aspirants.

(4) While we are still alive in this physical world, and possess a body, it exercises considerable influence on a man's psyche and even his mind. If it is ailing, manifestations of a man's powers may suffer, except when he is already a 'Liberated One' or accomplished Master. Sometimes such Great Beings incarnate in order to help and serve their younger brethren, that is, the rest of us. As the *Law of sacrifice* is the supreme one and transcends all other laws, Masters usually perform it to the utmost, that is, they make their departure from their physical bodies (death, as we say) the *summit of their sacrifice*, for our benefit. The story of Christ is too well known to be repeated here, but the Maharshi followed in the steps of his great predecessors and also accepted a unique sacrifice, which tortured his body for *more than a year*, thereby alleviating the karmas of those round him, but undoubtedly the true extent of his redemptory action was much greater, and is beyond our perception.

(5) If a man has a very burdened physical karma, it will hit him strongest when he makes attempts to gain spiritual enlightenment. This is *no* malicious joke from the side of a cruel power, but a normal and logical consequence. One cannot progress considerably if one still has to pay a heavy *prarabdha karma* (that is, that part which is destined to be consumed in the present incarnation). Therefore, attachment to a special path often precipitates a rain-like series of disasters and distress upon the head of such an aspirant. Now, if he is able to support all these difficulties, he wins and then quickly marches ahead.

But often it is not so and a man becomes broken and unable to do any further study. Such circumstances are what are known as 'karmic brakes'. They are very hard to resist and remove. That is why Christ in His Prayer instructs us to say: 'And lead us not into temptation.'

It is accepted in occult circles, that without active assistance from a genuine spiritual Master of the particular epoch, it is impossible to fight against adverse *prarabdha*.

* * * *

Now we will pass on to the next meditation verse, which belongs to this chapter.

Verse 4: *My true I-Self begins there, where all the activity of my mind-brain ends.*

We know that the final Samadhi (of the *Nirvikalpa, or formless type*) goes parallel with the developing of Self-knowledge in man. This produces the fact, that even some otherwise competent authors link the two together, that is, the *final Samadhi* and *Self-Realization* as one conception. Correctly speaking, from the practical point of view, both of them *melt* into the one at the end of the Path, so the absolute perennial Realization and Sahaja Samadhi are one and the same supreme (Fourth) state. But from our point of view, until the glorious aim is reached, the two currents may still be distinguished and separated to a certain degree. This means that some aspirants may be more susceptible to raising their consciousness to Samadhi than to Self-knowledge, and vice versa.

But for both types, the cessation of all mental activities is the principal condition, as Verse 4 tells us. Anyway, it is so logical, that the student should not have any difficulties in meditating about this verse successfully and without any trace of doubt, and so rise into the realm above and beyond the mind. Then you will *know* what your true essence is.

Verse 5 : *Who am I?*

This verse is none other than the famous *Vichara* or Self-Inquiry as given by the Master Maharshi. It is the weapon which can break all the obstacles on the Path of the lucky aspirant, who knows how to use it. In its outer form the Vichara still belongs to the realm of the mind, but its true contents, when submitted to the process of spiritual distillation, lose their words and become the *Power*, which takes the aspirant straight into the realm of the *Self*. Remember how the Maharshi, wishing to explain this mystery to his inquirers, did it in the form of a great simile, comparing the Vichara to the stick which sets the funeral pyre alight (see Chapter XIV), consequently it too is consumed together with the pyre. Evidently nothing remains of the ego-personality, which perishes in the fire of Self-Realization. This is the final answer to Self-Inquiry. The Master also told us : 'The answer to Vichara is the egoless state.' This is another form of the foregoing simile : when the ego perishes, all imperfections and evil go with it for ever and cannot be restored, just as we cannot again produce the corpse or the firewood from the consumed funeral pyre.

Meditation or incessant repetition of Vichara in your mind, with the effort to penetrate into the silent and wordless mystery of your Self, is the best known weapon against all failures and karmic onslaughts. This will be the final meditation to conclude this chapter.

Chapter XVII

The Motive Power of Hope

Verse 153: 'When the five sheaths are removed the pure *pratyagatman* (the Logos), the eternal happiness, all-pervading, the supreme self-generated light shines forth.'

THIS time let us put the question quite openly: 'Can you walk on the Path without any hope of reaching your aim?' So, Hope is one of the foremost powers, parallel to will-power, which make our aims attainable. Meditate about these conceptions until you utterly absorb them, without any shadow of doubt. This will also be a part of the initiation leading, together with the others, to Samadhi.

After that we come to a further analysis. Hope can be described as intuitional anticipation of a happy solution to an important problem in us. In this case the problem concerns the most precious thing we can imagine: our own being, our true I and not any temporary shell-personality, together with the body, for both will be dissolved without any trace in the future, merely passing into the dead past. When I say 'dead' I mean it. An example will explain this best.

Consider some person you knew and of whom you are the only survivor, say, your grandfather or other late relative. You have no doubt that he existed, perhaps a long time ago. You might know his personality, his outer form, his character. When everyone else who knew him has disappeared, no one will know anything about him, apart from yourself, who is still living, and in whose brain there are still those clichés of the past. But that is all. When you die, then nothing will remain of those memories. And the man (your relative) is completely erased from the picture of the incessantly changing world. The next step will be a clear anticipation of the same position applying to yourself. Quietly think about the unavoidable end of everything manifested, yourself included. It is not only thinking, but is a serious process in consciousness, directed to making easier the separation from that perishable form called the body.

You will experience this when practising these exercises, as reading alone can by no means be conclusive proof.

An unripe person will rather shun such mental processes, but others will find them very useful. After all, nobody can live through your life, and your *experiences* also belong to you alone. Therefore, you are entitled to operate with them according to your needs.

Returning to the subject of this chapter, we see where we should not place our hope under any circumstances: *in that which perishes, disappears.* For there are, as in everything in this world, two sides to Hope: a right and a wrong one, hope for a wise person and for a fool. Remember that all these chapters of Parts I to III are preparation for Samadhi. They operate for you as you still *are*, a relative being, not yet transformed into *That* which arises as the supreme Sun of the final Superconsciousness. Therefore relative methods may be used for relative things. Self-Inquiry is the unique and positive form in which the *search* can be conducted. The classical method, so far used in Hindu Vedanta, must be, and is negative, and briefly, is contained in the formula 'Neti! Neti!' (Not this! Not this!). We should not underestimate its value just because we know about the Vichara. The Self-Inquiry cannot be used by everyone. The Maharshi himself, while recommending Vichara as a means *par excellence*, always issued a warning, that we should not be mistaken and imagine that it will bring us Realization of the Self as if on a plate. The negative method of the gradual 'peeling' off of our shells from the central *light* within us, by meditation about our bodies and attitudes, applying 'Neti! Neti!' to all of them, is much easier for, and more accessible to the great majority of aspirants, except those who have had the privilege to sit at the feet of a true Master of Self-Realization, as the Maharshi was for our age.

To be in the Self, to realize It, is to retain only the consciousness of the Self, that is, of absolute, attributeless, illimitable Being. It is equally possible for an incarnate or disincarnate man. But for experiencing it for the *first* time, the primary Realization must be performed while one still has a bodily form. Later, it becomes immaterial, but the beginning must be made on this earth. This rule affects all human attainments, so there is little to expect from the post-incarnation periods of life and the main lessons must be taken beforehand.

Verse 6: *Now I am creating the stillness in my mind. I have no desire to think any more.*

This meditation and all the following ones are different from Verses 1 to 5. They deal with the active effort of the aspirant, who has to reform his consciousness, shifting it closer to the final aim—Samadhi. In this verse we still our mind, as a forerunner to transcending it. As we know from the second book of the Trilogy (*Concentration*), the stilling and emptying of the mind is possible only as a successful result of passive concentration, which is a much more difficult form. But it is the *key*, the *condition*, the '*sine qua non*' for every successful attempt when climbing to the heights of Samadhi.

More than sixty years ago the first practical exponent of Hindu Yoga for the West, Swami Vivekananda (a gifted disciple of the great Saint Ramakrishna), tried to unify the then existing different yogic methods for physical and all further development. He simplified them by advocating the following pattern:

(a) Twelve *Dharanas* (breathing exercises with fixation of the mind, similar to those given in *Concentration* as pranayamas) will constitute one *Dhyana*.

(b) Twelve *Dhyanas* are equal to *Samadhi*.

We disagree with this over-simplification in techniques and theory, as we now have more extensive information about the true meaning of the Supreme State of Nirvikalpa Samadhi. It is *not* sufficient to perform 144 Dharanas (which is extremely hard to achieve anyway) in order to find oneself in pure Superconsciousness. The foremost authority in all matters concerning Samadhi and Self-Realization, the Great Rishi Ramana, never taught that Attainment might be a result of, or dependent upon *asanas* (postures of the body in Dharana for example) or rhythmical breathing. He separated yogic exercises from the growth of spirituality in man. When opportune he would say, that when the mind is absorbed in the Light of the Self (in other words, when it temporarily enters into Kevala Nirvikalpa), breathing automatically becomes rhythmical. And when the immersion reaches its climax, the breath stops completely. From this fact, some not-so-competent exponents of Yoga have concluded, that if they will breathe rhythmically for a long time and then stop it, they must enter into Samadhi.

But these processes are *not* at all reversible, and this explains why so much bungling and unfulfilled prescriptions can be found in books written by compilers who have never been able to practise what they wrote.

Nevertheless, for many aspirants, the stilling of the mind becomes easier if they try to breathe rhythmically, but without any hard effort, just as advised in *Concentration*, Part III.

The second half of Verse 6 requires still more of the aspirant: he should have *no desire* to think any more. It seems to be unattainable, as thinking is apparently inherent in one's mind. This is true, *but actually the mind is not inherent in you!* Who says that mind is indispensable to the *Self*? Only those who know nothing better and higher. And only those who still identify themselves (consciously or subconsciously) with their thinking processes and the tool—the brain in the physical body. We already know that such an

127

attitude is an obstacle which must be removed. 'Well, so says the theory,' you may object. But how to reach this in practice, how to realize it? Both parts of this verse are in full harmony and interdependent. If you still your mind, it will enter into a peculiar state, in which you can *see* it (mind) in its suspension, while the *consciousness* now apart from it, expands itself beyond the muddy waves of the mental ocean. Realize this first in theory with your intellect.

Now another law comes into action which rules the consciousness at this height. When you reach (even for a short time) full independence from the processes of feeling and thinking, you then have *no desire* to live any more in the lower worlds, that is, on the astromental level.

Your natural intention then, is to remain in that blessed land of peace and fulfilment. Just as you cognize something better than your usual and normal conditions, so you will always try to retain that higher standard instead of the former lower one. As you see, the solution is simple and logical, and fully attainable. The wonder of the magnificent attainments of the great saints now becomes more understandable. From a certain level up, they have a powerful attraction for the *heights* as, unfortunately, average men rather have for the lowlands. This may be likened to physical mountains and valleys. At a certain distance from the surface of a planet gravity ceases to exert a downward pull, and in these new conditions the physical object can be attracted by other celestial bodies. But this *critical height must be attained* before the law can operate.

So, in order to lose the desire for thinking, one must first taste the bliss of the state of freedom from thoughts. A dish cannot be appreciated until it has been tasted. What can be clearer than this?

The idea of Hope, which is called the *motive force of Attainment*, when connected with the meditation of Verse 6, leads to the following conception:

If we realize this verse through our own endurance in the fulfilment of its instruction, our Hope will turn into Attainment. This was, is and will be the aim of this mystical force.

Verse 7: *Now the sky of my consciousness is pure. There are no cloud-thoughts in it.*

This is another aspect of Verse 6. The most difficult things for true and full Realization are just the simplest ones. We can freely wander in the vast forests of the multiple conceptions of mind, theories and problems. This may please our mind, give it new fuel as material for thinking, and allow it to vibrate full scale as this force likes to do first and foremost. Present-day humanity is enslaved by mind. But can we affirm that this slavery has brought it any happiness? From our point of view, this age is affected by great errors: the tool has been accepted as the master, and the true doer has been removed to second place, nay, utterly forgotten.

On the physical plane, according to the ever true Hermetic maxim 'As above so below', and vice versa, similar things have happened. Fifty years ago we lived without the innumerable gadgets, plastics, new means of communication, luxury of technical boons, and so on, but also without 'H' bombs and without the constant fear of a sudden annihilating catastrophe, against which we are completely defenceless and helpless, as it hangs over our heads like the sword of Damocles. And we cannot do anything, for while only soldiers fought in the field before, now whole nations are recognized as targets for destruction.

Just as mental processes alone cannot bring us the *Wisdom*, which is beyond the limited knowledge of mind, as well as its possibilities, so years of incredible materialistic progress have not been able to put us any closer to happiness, to anything worthy of this name in either social or political harmony. The attentive student will undoubtedly discover the true cause of such misfortune in this epoch: immense and rapidly growing, reckless materialism, which directs all the efforts and abilities of the human population of this planet to the comfort and service of the body-ego, so that little remains for anything else. The results follow unmistakably.

This planet is not a dead thing. Western occultism knows a lot about the great being, whose physical body is our earth. Perhaps we cannot understand such a life, as is that of a planet, but we can feel some fearsome reactions from its side. Here I mean the convulsions of the earth's skin, costing so many lives and bringing destruction to those tiny beings, who like insects, inhabit the surface of the globe. Some occultists believe that earth does not like the nuclear explosions very much, which go deep into its body and the ominous growling of earthquakes may be the last warning. But earth, like ourselves, is not omnipotent and is not allowed to do everything it wishes. There are forces which control the microcosmos as well as the macrocosmos. Otherwise we would long ago have ceased to exist (see *The Tarot*).

* * * *

In this Verse 7, thoughts are called 'clouds'. For those who possess the experimental knowledge of the higher states of consciousness this is an open truth. The Maharshi taught that all misery and unhappiness come from the mind and its restless thoughts. When they are removed the horizon is pure like a cloudless sky. But under the term 'mind' he understood just what is used in Advaita: all the functions based on the conception of relativity and the personality-ego.

Here there is a warning: some people, otherwise utterly untrained in concentration, say that they have periods when they cannot find any thoughts in their minds. Is this what we are seeking in this study? Of course *not!* The more primitive the individual man, the more *'dolce far niente'* occurs in his mind-brain. This is not that inner freedom and independence from compulsory thinking which—if duly developed—is a precursor of Samadhi: it is simply stagnation of the mental functions. We do not seek for it.

After being deliberately switched off, the dominated mind works perfectly, like a sharp and well-preserved tool in the hands of a good craftsman.

So, these 'clouds' should be removed when we do not need them. This is possible only when there is power in us, independent of the mind which can, and will obey our will. And this power in us is always looking on its tools, as upon *separate* things. This is the *initiation* of Verse 7.

Verse 8: *Now I am free. I am beyond all.*

The hope of being free is the most enlightening striving in man. This verse tells us that this can be an accomplished fact. Now, really meditate:

When the mind is stilled there is no desire to think any more. We become free when there are no clouds covering the horizon of our purified consciousness. Perfect freedom cannot be limited by any limitations coming just from thoughts, born, in turn, from inner desires. In the Hindu Scriptures the desireless man is called just the 'liberated one' or Jivanmukta. If there are desires there cannot be any perfection or freedom. So this is where we find the logical explanation of those apparently abstruse qualities, ascribed to the *men* who reached the end of the Path. That is why Samadhi—in which there are no needs or desires—is called the state of absolute bliss. The bliss of realized eternity, which the writer saw in the eyes of his Master.

After you have assimilated the meditation of the first half of Verse 8, the second follows easily and clearly.

I am beyond all. This 'all' is, of course, everything 'outside' of *That*, of the pure consciousness I am. If you are free, it means only that you are really beyond all bonds and forms. Nothing can be added to the immaterial, ever free *I-Self*, just as you cannot add water to fire, because it will evaporate. And so evaporates every shell, desire and thought facing the *Self*. There is no further place for them in the fire of Spirit.

Here fire symbolizes the eternal indestructible consciousness-Self, it cannot be extinguished by any amount of the water called Maya.

It can only be shadowed, or shrouded and veiled, and this is the case of evolution as was explained in previous chapters. Another meaning of the term 'beyond' may signify that when free, we are inaccessible to any attachments from 'below'. The nature of that 'below' is described for us in the next verse.

Verse 9: *I am beyond my bodies and the whole planet.*

This means that the shrouds of matter of different density and quality have no more attraction for the liberated person. Physically, no material or fleshly form attracts the consciousness *set free.*

In Eastern Scriptures it is said that the wise man looks with an equal eye on everything: small or large, beautiful or ugly, good or bad. Nothing affects him, for what he sees as a manifestation is only a temporary veil, which will soon be dissipated like the morning mist. And there is nothing in common between that which such a Sage is and these veils (and he knows it). In the Bhagavad Gita it is directly stated, that Sages are *not* affected by life or death, and that these do not worry them. This is because they are in Samadhi, beyond both states, which affect only the shells but not the essence. If we identify ourselves with these shells, the responsibility, ignorance and suffering is our business.

It seems to be easy to accept all this mentally (as theory), but it is *not* sufficient. The 'Essence' must be realized as one's true being, the immutable Core. The answer to Vichara, which is the instrument of that search is, of course, the discovery of It, born from persistent and well directed meditations. There are occultists who bluntly say that the answer to Vichara is only *I am.* If one prefers to clothe everything in words, such solution of the Self-Inquiry would be acceptable. Anyway even the Master Maharashi once said that the biblical formula of God: '*I am that I am*' depicts the *whole truth* as can be attempted to express it in speech. The final meditation for this chapter will be:

Verse 10: *They* (that is, my bodies and the whole planet) *do not exist any more, for they were only a dream of my mind.*

It is the final blow to the conception of Maya in us. The very existence of forms is denied. Is this so? Analyse things for yourself: philosophically, and according to occult conceptions, as well as those of Advaita-Vedanta, existence means *something which Is.* (1) Not that which *was* before and ceased to be. (2) Not that which *is* now, but will cease to be. (3) Not that which *was* and *is*, but will cease to be in the future. And finally (4) Not that which will be and will pass away like the three former conditions.

Some hard work may be needed in order to meditate through and to digest these definitions, belonging to the little word *Is.*

The synthesis made in words of these four definitions will be simple: the *Is*, the *Existence* means the attitude which we call 'eternal'. From this point of view (the only one which has value for the seekers of Samadhi), it is clear that our bodies, those of everyone else and the planet's, together with the apparent universe, do not possess, and *cannot* possess the pure attribute of *Existence*. Hope, the power which motivates us to seek and thereby allows us to find, is *not* directed to any of the conceptions which are incompatible with our now explained term of *being*, of true *Existence*, of *Is*.

In Samadhi this existence is realized and lived. That is why It was, and is so eagerly sought after by advanced souls, and so glorified by those who have found this *state*, in which, as the ancient Sages of India say, they *are able to see the whole apparently infinite universe as if in a drop of water*. Meditate about this!

The mind may refuse to accept such revolutionary statements, but they are not directed to it. They belong to *that in you*, which *Is*. What more can be said?

*   *   *   *

What is the true origin of Hope? This power is mostly used unconsciously, as a ready result of some unknown factors. In our opinion these factors can be: a flash of *intuition* (knowledge without thinking) in us, plus a dimmed awareness of our karma's clichés. Anyway both can be found if you analyse a personal example, that is, a case where you had or have a reasonable hope for your future. Hope is a positive force, and in their theological philosophy and dogmas, the Fathers of the early Church in the first centuries of Christianity, placed Hope equal with two other cardinal virtues, without which there is no salvation: *Faith* and *Love*.

That Hope possesses motive-power is clear because no reasonable man would undertake any major work or step without hope of fulfilling it successfully. And so it is with this study: would you try earnestly if there is no hope in you of being successful?

In our lives we often pass too lightly over many words which actually have great meaning, once we are able to discover it. As an example, we can take the conception of *Faith* standing alongside that of Hope. Do you know the exact meaning of this word apart from the popular one, used in ordinary language?

In occultism, *Faith* is also recognized as a *great power* and the saying of Christ about the faith which can move mountains is fully confirmed in the Western Tradition, and the words of the Great Teacher are recognized as *realizable Truth*.

Many people know from their own experience that any work or

endeavour performed with faith in its success has quite a different meaning from work that is poisoned from the beginning by uncertainty and doubt. This particularly refers to all spiritual searching and many eminent occultists firmly consider that no realization can be obtained if the aspirant is only a prey to his doubts, and therefore has no faith.

Chapter XVIII

Hostile Forces on the Path

Verse 162: ' "I am the body"—such is the opinion of a deluded man; of the learned the notion of I is in relation to the body, as well as to the *Jiva* (monad). Of the great soul possessed of discrimination and direct perception, "I am Brahman", such is the conviction with regard to the eternal self.'

WE usually begin our study, as we are while still existing in the realm of relativity, and using relative forces, until we see the end of the Path. It can even be said, that the foremost efforts of every aspirant are made just in this relative world, despite the fact that in his *Core* (spiritual heart as the Maharshi called it) he must have the bright spark of the *Absolute Light*, a reflection of the true Samadhi that is to be gained. When there is relativity, there must be light and shade. They both help to create the actual picture of the manifested universe in which we spend our incarnations.

In plain language it can be said that: *good* and *evil*, friends and foes, light and darkness, happiness and misery, love and hatred, and many other binaries of this type are included among the problems which must be solved by every disciple on the Path, for he will encounter them all and will have to 'neutralize' them in his own life. It is impossible in a study of this class, destined to show the path to the *Consciousness of the Future*—as Samadhi is often called in occult circles—to give such exact instructions for the aspirant, as has been done in *Concentration*, which operates first and foremost with the mind, that is, with a force which we can, and must dominate. But here the search is not for the relative, but for the innermost, absolute *Core*-being of man.

In a study such as this, the writer is not confronted solely by less experienced students who want to be taught. Reflections, or germs of Samadhi must already be manifested, albeit in an infinitesimal degree, in the disciple. This changes the whole picture of the instructions. Therefore, the main task of the writer is to provide material which, in the past, has been useful for others, so that it may be helpful for present aspirants. But *the way* in which he expounds the qualities necessary for a successful finalizing of the Path is his own concern. That is why, in this book, there are no numbered exercises and time-tables. If there were they would be useful for only one person of definite abilities and point of view, that is for the writer himself.

To use a simile, different foods can be offered on plates, but it is you who have to choose and consume them. We can now pass on to the contents proper of this chapter, in the hope that the meaning of the foregoing is clear to you.

There cannot and will not be any difficulties if you encounter friendly forces on your path. They assist in many ways, and arrange things so that the aspirant has no doubts from where the help comes. Consequently, there is no need to discuss it.

But things are different if shadows and hostile influences appear on the Path. This is more than probable, because of the nature of the constitution of the relative universe, composed as it is of light and shade.

The first hostile elements you may face will be if you speak to indifferent persons about your study and aims. They may try to ridicule you in order to shatter your decision and endurance. Why do some people act like this? We have to be aware of a fact well known to occult psychology (but not necessarily to the official one), that the majority of average, that is, undeveloped men do not like to see any-one advancing and obtaining a higher status than themselves. Un-fortunately this ugly and nonsensical sort of jealousy very often flowers amongst us, and the hostile forces take advantage to use it in full. These forces do not come with horns and forks to spill hot tar and pitch on you ! They act in a hidden way, sometimes too hard to discover, and therefore to identify. If the average man knew that he had become a tool of the powers of darkness, he would probably think twice before he committed an evil act. Anyway, it is the responsibility of the student himself, to act wisely and not to provide any oppor-tunity in which to be harmed. In such a case, he himself must share at least half the guilt for the besetting troubles. He should not discuss his intimate, spiritual endeavour with others, except those engaged like himself on a similar search, or those who know more about the Path than he does. Men will always be hostile to anything which they cannot understand in other people, especially if it is a 'mysterious study', a Yoga, and so on. They will try to belittle what they feel is beyond their own reach. The wise aspirant will take account of this and act accordingly. There is no other choice. You cannot change the world, but you can and must change yourself.

The next kind of obstacles can come from your as yet unexhausted karma. When we engage ourselves in a study such as this, we are actually challenging our past errors and debts which still have to be rectified and paid. In plain language, this means that you might be called upon to pay for them earlier and in much larger amounts than your normal *Prarabdha* would otherwise require, just like instalments for goods bought on terms. If you want to be free from the burden earlier, you have to increase the amount of the instalments thereby shortening the time of repayment. So, do not seek any alleviation in your karma just because you are engaged in an incontestably 'good' work—an intense search for the great inheritance of the future—Samadhi, the new consciousness, which others will attain in later ages. Now realize the origin of the apparent hostility of your karma and be at peace.

Probably it would be interesting for you to know, even approximately, what forms the opposition is likely to take. Its resistance may manifest itself in several ways. It is, of course, impossible to mention all of them, because of their innumerable variety. But in general it can be mentioned as follows :

(a) Conditions in one's family which, in the first years, prevent one from having a certain amount of the solitude necessary for meditation, and lack of means to provide better conditions.

(b) Weak health which does not permit greater mental strain, unavoidable in efforts to practise concentration.

(c) Excessive business activities, where the outer world's influences do not allow enough time for exercises or meditation, when one becomes too tired at the end of one's working day to perform any additional task.

(d) Direct resistance from one's closest environment, such as relatives, associates, and so on.

All these can, and must be overcome. Enough good will, firm determination to do what has been recognized as the only worthy aim of one's life, intelligent handling of circumstances and finally, the invisible aid usually granted to those who satisfy the requisite qualities, may balance the opposition and leave enough room for the Path in the given incarnation.

If things turn out differently, and you cannot find any possible solution, accept it as a sign that this Path is premature for you and then seek another one. In any case, if you will firmly try simply to become a *good human being*, and if you carry out this decision in your everyday life, the Path will be closer to you with every day, until an unmistakable sign will open the mysterious door to it.

There are other forces, which may oppose your efforts on the first plane, and these are the *involutionary astral currents*. You might be assaulted by outbursts of emotions and feelings which come to your consciousness and try to occupy it for their own purposes (see *Concentration*, Chapter X).

They may literally *tempt* you in order to attract your attention, which is a life-giving force for them, as well as for the next obstacles, those of mental origin.

Thoughts may start to storm your brain, one apparently more urgent and 'important' than another, not allowing you to find the inner silence for a successful meditation. All these currents come from certain astro-mental centres in the universe, *which are aware* of human efforts aimed at the achievement of the Superconsciousness, that is, to become their ruler and independent of them, as well as from any outer influences. I would not like to call these forces 'diabolic', as some other authors do, although they are definitely hostile to evolutionary strivings in us. Christ told us: 'The Spirit is willing, but the flesh is weak.' Under this body of flesh an occultist will recognize all three sheaths which envelop the consciousness of the *Self-Spirit*, that is the physical, astral and mental counterparts in us. It is useless for our present purpose to seek for these 'whys', inquiring about the causes of such a state of things. Moreover, the explanations cannot be given in terms accessible to and operative for the average mind. But those who can raise their self-awareness into the formless region beyond the mind's realm, *know* the causes.

Until we are able to do the same, the simple fact that '*it is so and not otherwise*' must suffice for us. There is no other solution at this time. Later, everything is solved of itself, and advanced people have no questions or doubts at all. This is the hope of every earnest student, and *this hope will never be frustrated*.

In the beginning, some aspirants to the Path have to suffer extremely intensive attacks from the side of the above-mentioned currents, bringing them impure emotions of great force and lots of restless thoughts in apparently never-ending streams. The only real weapons against these obstacles are: (1) Endurance and a strong will to persevere in your efforts. (2) Deep realization of the justice of your strivings. (3) Turning to the supporting 'good' forces for assistance. It can be reached, for example, by some theurgic means like sincere prayers directed to the *impersonal source* of all goodness and purity, which we call—God. Technical means which have also proved to be effective are indicated in full detail in *Concentration*, Part III, and there is no reason to quote them again in these pages.

For those of you who have preserved an intuitional belief in the great Son of Man whom we call the Christ, and who know the mystical power of the sign of the Cross, when made on the believer himself, may benefit from its following use.

Firstly, as usual, place the joined fingers of your right hand on your forehead, pronouncing slowly and concentrating on these words: 'In the name of the Father' (think about the infinite, unknown, absolute Source of everything); then lower your hand to the solar plexus, pronouncing in the same way the words 'of the Son crucified for us'. Here intensive inner work is necessary. Think about the immense sacrifice of the *Son of Man*, who suffered for all human beings in order to alleviate their burdens and pains. Realize this as being related to all periods past, present and future alike. And then, the most important moment of the whole operation, *include* yourself and your actual difficulties among those benefited by the Sacrifice on the Cross. Feel this, as if you were present at it.

There is hardly anything more to add. Whoever is able, will realize and follow the stream of Grace which comes from the Cross for all those who turn to It.

Next, place your hand on one of your shoulders with the words: 'and Holy Ghost', meditating on the omniprescence and omnipotence of Its Effulgence. Finally, put you hand on the other shoulder, with 'Amen' in your mind. This will be a confirmation of the whole operation.

Certain Christian Saints used a special prayer or invocation to the most mysterious Person of the Holy Trinity—the Holy Spirit. Its power guarded them from all attacks, menacing, as we know, those who advance beyond others.

O Ruler of Heaven, Consoler and Spirit of Truth!
Who abides everywhere and fills everything,
Giver of Life, come unto us and dwell in us.
Cleanse us from every impurity and save our souls
O merciful Lord!

Some occultists used the sign of the Cross, as mentioned above, even against physical ailments, and made it effective by operating with their *faith*. In the second phase of making the sign of the Cross, when they pronounced 'of the Son', they placed their hand on the affected part of their body, such as the chest, eyes, abdomen, and so on, remembering that the *Crucified One* was subjected to every kind of pain on His cross. If this mystical link between the Crucified and the praying believer has been really established by faith and devotion, results come in the form of an instant cure.

Prayer can be greatly fortified by certain theurgic methods. One of the best and most used among occultists is as follows. Before beginning to pray, remember that prayer was, and is continuously rising from many highly developed men like saints, as powerful currents from earth to heaven. I have used symbols here, hoping that they will be clear for the reader. Now, *add* your own prayers, melting them (in imagination) in the ascending, luminous currents produced by the Saints. Briefly, *associate yourself with them.* If your admiration and recognition for them is sincere, the results of your prayer, performed in this way, will be astonishing, and the purification produced in your consciousness will be very effective and real.

The prayer to the Holy Ghost (as given above) is particularly suitable for this theurgic operation, as it was, and is, used by many highly evolved humans.

Of course, the Lord's Prayer can also be used successfully in the same way. Another example of theurgic action will be the mystical prayer by the Eastern Saints and directed to *God the Father* (the Highest Unmanifested Principle).

'O Lord, teach me always to fulfil Thy Will.'

Every prayer should be well meditated through before being put into action, so that the maximum benefit may be obtained.

In the Eastern Church a formula is used to strengthen the prayer and give it mystical power. Occultists also know about this addition used before every individual prayer, which is: '*Through the prayers of Thy Saints.*' After what has been mentioned about our association with the Saints' prayers, there is no need for much explanation concerning this form of theurgy. Who actually are the men whom we call Saints? To a layman, they are very good men, who do not commit any sins, and who have access to the Almighty, while for a scientifically minded occultist, besides being a good man, a Saint is also a wise one, who has practical knowledge of that which we suppose to be merely a theory: the relation of the microcosm to the macrocosm, or of man to God. It is a wonderful state. On one side, such a being, like ourselves, has a body and its needs, while on the other, the Saint lives in the realm of the Spirit (that is, God) and has no doubts about it. He is a bridge between earth and heaven, as some pious men say. The unwise opinion that everyone has access to the Highest is ridiculous, for as Bernard Shaw wisely said: 'the conversion of a savage to Christianity is really the conversion of Christianity to savagery.'

An undeveloped consciousness cannot even imagine the heights on which dwells the *All*, in Its splendour and absoluteness. The very idea of this is beyond the perception of the vast majority of present-day humanity. So how could they 'see' God?

That is why, those who know more, honour the advanced sons of humanity, whose evolution is far beyond that of the average level.

In a Saint, a Hermetist, finds the temporary solving of a very difficult binary: life in matter and in Spirit. The absolute solution is the annihilation of this binary in the fire of the *Orb of Full Light* (see Chapter XXII). Therefore it is accepted that every contact with such advanced beings, as are the Saints, is helpful and benefactory for us. The prayers of the Saints have no personal or egoistic intentions. They know about the unity of Life, and they pray for all and everything. The wise aspirant will use such opportunities for his own progress. This is the meaning of the sentence about the 'Prayers of Thy Saints'.

*   *   *   *

In this or another way, one has to fight against inimical forces when they appear to act against us. Who will win this struggle against the currents delaying our achievement? He who can display more power, as well as secure protection from the *positive source* as mentioned in the first part of this chapter. Among the 'mixed' obstacles, whose origin is simultaneously in our own physical, astral and mental counterparts, the following may be mentioned:

(a) Sleepiness which systematically overwhelms some aspirants as soon as they begin meditation and other exercises. The weapon against this will be to give the body a little more sleep, thereby removing the possible physical cause of the evil. Then use the force of your will, rejecting sleepiness which becomes unreasonable, when the body has been given enough rest in the normal time.

However, it is known, that advanced occultists and saints have limited their sleep to a few hours daily, and have still been able to make every spiritual effort they wished and needed. Their developed will-power helped them.

(b) A more serious hostile phenomenon may be disturbed sleep in the night. Some people on the Path have to endure this obstacle when sleeplessness appears, usually about 2 or 3 a.m. after only a few hours rest. A man may feel perfectly healthy, and still have to spend hours until morning in fighting the assaulting thoughts, which prevent him from sleeping.

There are several recommended remedies.

(1) A cold shower before retiring, between 10 and 11 p.m. is best. In stubborn cases, the body should be washed with a wet towel, leaving no portion of the skin dry. The whole operation should not take longer than one minute. Then immediately go to bed *without* drying the body, but using enough blankets to warm up well beneath them.

(2) Not to go to sleep earlier than two hours after the last meal.

(3) When in bed, pronounce the sacred syllable 'Aum', counting the repetitions until falling asleep.

(4) When awakened in the middle of the night and having difficulty in returning to sleep, use No. 3 as a remedy.

(5) The powerful exorcism given in *Concentration*, Chapter IX, used like a mantra will also be helpful.

(6) Sometimes nightmares persecute the aspirant. They come from unsuitable astral conditions, when the body lies sleeping and the astrosome begins to live its proper life—in the astral plane. If this happens and the dreams become connected with fear, two weapons may be used against it. The first is the previously mentioned exorcism. The second, a firm mental repetition, with full concentration of *I am*. This must be *lived* with the understanding that *I am* means the true *existence* which cannot be affected by anything and therefore is beyond all dangers and fears. In order to be effective both formulas should be exercised (repeated mentally, and when possible aloud) in the day time, that is, when you are awake and can well memorize them. Gradually both will pass, as intended, into the dream state and will work there for you, every time that you need strength, self-confidence and fearlessness on the astral and mental planes.

These difficulties and troubles, as described, may appear at the time of your work towards the enlargement of consciousness, because then we may become more sensitive to astro-mental influences. As we are still imperfect from many points of view, they may be the lower vibrations and beings from these two not normally perceivable worlds, which approach us, for then (that is, when we exercise) we attract their attention. There is no real danger in these phenomena, but our individual reactions may be improper and therefore harmful to our psychology and even health.

An occult law is that if our consciousness functions normally (in the waking state) on a certain plane, then, when asleep, we should be conscious in the next higher plane and so function in it. Now you may understand why, in preparation for Samadhi (which is beyond the mental plane), we try to dominate and subdue the reflections of the astral and mental planes in ourselves. I deliberately say *in ourselves* and *not* in the whole world surrounding us. It is unnecessary for our direct purpose, but certain types of occultism also occupy themselves with these two higher planes and their inhabitants. In the search of the real, highest and final Consciousness (Samadhi) we simply do not need any manifestations of Maya, no matter if we call them physical, astral or mental, for all are only temporal illusions,

141

unworthy to be our aim. The Sage Maharshi told us that: 'What is not permanent will be lost, and what will be lost is not worth striving for.' How logical and clear is this conception, but it is convincing and guiding only for ripe minds. With this we will end the direct account of the hostile forces which we can encounter on the Path, passing on to the active part of the study, the next verses for meditation.

Verse 11 : *Now I am awakened from that dream.*

If you attentively followed the means given in this chapter against hostile forces, when encountered along the Path, it should not escape your attention that these means are directed against just those 'dreams of your mind' as are all visions, apparitions, theories and other astro-mental activities not connected with our higher Principle (the immaterial imperishable and unattached-to-anything *Self*), but with our mortal, ego-personality. So our next problem is to finish with unworthy dreaming in the mental plane. Since he is living, and is primarily conscious on the physical plane, the average man terms his astral experiences dreams, that is, things which are unreal, and which only appear and disappear. Consequently, such an attitude is not wrong, but for us it should be extended further to the mental plane, that realm of the mind. We have to be awakened beyond mind, and then we will have the full right to call it *illusion*, as did, and do all the great initiated Sages and Teachers of humanity. The task is neither a light nor an easy one. The *true approach* is, like everything in Part III, only *proper meditation*, and applies to this and all the other verses given here for your use. To awaken from a dream means to become aware of reality, cognizing, at the same time, the illusory character of everything else, which cannot be put into the category of the *Real*, that is, *Existence* as was explained in Chapter XVII. Think about this in full inner peace and analyse what, in you, belongs to the *Real* and what to Maya, using the gradual 'peeling' or 'rejecting' process. Considerable inner progress will be made if you follow this advice exactly.

Verse 12 : *There is nothing around me, only infinite space.*

This is an extension of Verse 11, which allows us to go deeper and deeper into *active, realizable meditation*. In this we are rejecting *everything*, for this 'everything' is all untruth, having no existence, But something should be done in order to allow you 'to breathe' in this apparent 'nothingness'. And to our aid comes '*only infinite space*'. This can be realized through the higher regions of mortal consciousness. Imagine that you are in *space*, empty and extending infinitely on all sides. But do *not verbalize*, rather visualize, if you like this conception. Be immobile, desireless, without any trace of that tragic extraversion of the mind, which persistently spoils innumerable incarnations of our brethren who want to live without knowing what is the real life. Be in the 'centre' of the *Great Space*. Sankaracharya also uses this way in his approach to Samadhi. I always prefer to follow the line of the *classical writers* of spiritual philosophy, for they really experienced what they taught, and they possessed *Wisdom*, while the ignorant masses, in the best of cases, strive only for temporary *knowledge*. This verse may duly remind you of the final exercise of Part III of *Concentration*. Then it was a hint, a suggestion of the existence of deeper experiences. Now you see for yourself that the time is coming to *realize* things, and not merely to think about them.

So, remain for as long as you can in the *centre*, with nothing around you, and enjoy the inherent bliss which is a faint foretaste of that which awaits you in the Orb of Full Light—in Kevala Nirvikalpa.

Verse 13 : *I am like this space—having no end.*

In the next, a great step forward, you are *not* the onlooker, gazing through the eyes of your subtle mind into the Space, symbolizing the Infinite and Eternity. You *are* It. You live It. There is no longer a symbol, but Realization itself. Think ! You are dissolved into the Space which has no end; is it not the absolute, final freedom in you? The bliss is again intensified. Perhaps, in these moments, in your purified consciousness you perceive what is *life* and what *immortality*. Remain in the meditation of being in the Space, for nothing more in words can be added to this experience.

When you return (perhaps unwillingly and with disgust) to your everyday, limited consciousness, *try to remind* yourself as often as you can of the first glimpses of *That*, even though it is impossible to express this by speech or thought. The actual value of this meditation and the ensuing experience, if you were successful, is that you will *know*, that there is the *Imperishable* which dwells in the heart of your inner Sanctuary.

Chapter XIX

The Rising Sun of Samadhi

Verse 134: 'This unmanifested spiritual consciousness begins to manifest like the dawn in the pure heart, and shining like the midday sun in the "cave of wisdom" illuminating whole universe.'

Verse 500: 'Like space I go further than thought (am all-pervading). Like the sun I am different from what is made visible (by it). Like a mountain I am eternally immovable. Like the ocean I am boundless.'

THE experiences connected with meditations along the lines of Verses 11 and 13 should finally bring a considerable extension of consciousness and the birth of new conceptions, not just theoretical ones which arise from the limited mind, but from the direct perception of things extending beyond the capacities of mind and thought. I remember the ecstatic words of Omar Khayyam when, under the veil of common language, he tried to convey the supreme idea of the spiritual rebirth in man:

'For a new Marriage I did make Carouse:
    Divorced old barren Reason [mind] from my bed,
And took the Daughter of the Vine to Spouse.'

Omar speaks clearly about the necessity of transcending the limited mind in order to ascend into the bliss of the pure, living consciousness above it. Not all of us can be poets, but this does not bar us from the same experience of Superconsciousness in Samadhi, when the hour of our ripeness arrives.

I will now speak about this sublime time to my earnest readers and principally to aspirants on the Path. The whole secret of Attainment lies in personal experience and not in the studying of so-called philosophical works, written under the dictates of the speculating mind, guessing and vacillating, which—according to the spiritual teaching of the great Masters like Christ, Buddha and Maharshi—is unable to *experience* Truth. Neatly expounded mental conceptions will flatter people enslaved by their minds, no matter how able these

144

minds may appear to be to us. But they are useless, and therein lies the whole tragedy. Take all Western philosophers: they created certain periods when some intellectuals were interested and perhaps admired their 'masters'; but at no time did things go beyond those limited circles. And it is so even today. But the most essential thing is, that all the thick volumes do not give any experience and the happiness inherent in it. Often the creators themselves of these mental theories and personal conceptions have been deeply unhappy men. This provides much food for thought for every keen intellectual. Of what use are even the most cleverly exposed mental combinations, when they are sterile and produce nothing more than temporary mental savours, leaving the cardinal question of every living being unsolved, and the inevitable end just as menacing and ominous as it was before? Even great religions bring much more real solace and inner harmony, and at least they are able to conjure away the old phantom of death.

There are cases where some purely mental theories and ideas (not experienced in their realizable value), when put into action, bring little of good to the nations or societies concerned. And even this 'little' is overwhelmed by the evil brought into force when the ignorant masses try to practise what, in its essence, surpasses their understanding. Then evil passions arise no longer limited in action by the now rejected former laws.

The Encyclopaedists of France in the eighteenth century supposedly had the best of intentions to reform the old, cumbersome regime and so give the masses more freedom and happiness, based on their mental deliberations and theories; but they were far removed from any experience and knowledge of the psychology of the lower classes, since they themselves were rather aristocrats.

But if subsequently they could have risen from their graves and seen the French Revolution with all its cruelty, murders, slavery and perversion, instead of the supposed freedom and happiness, which followed on from their well-intentioned books and pamphlets, they certainly would have destroyed them rather than let them be published.

Another example may be the practical results of the Russian Revolution of 1918, also apparently made in the name of liberation and social justice, but actually bringing poverty for the masses, coupled with slavery and terror so far unknown in human history.

Reformers should have something more than clever minds and theoretical skill if they hope to bring improvement instead of a worsening of conditions. An all round knowledge of man is needed, and not just that taken from the point of view of gross materialism.

In this book you have a non-religious and non-philosophical (in the sense mentioned in the previous paragraphs) approach to the deepest search which man can ever undertake, the search for his ultimate *Core*—the *imperishable* in himself. And this not by individual (and therefore doubtful) speculations, but by efforts to achieve the higher level of consciousness, which alone can solve problems which are far beyond the mind's powers and capacity. For us it is true that for the achievement of some physical and mental abilities we should put a lot of effort and work into them (for example gymnastics, physical as well as mental, degrees, and so on), just in the desired direction, that is of abilities, and *not* merely load the brain with considerable information and knowledge which has to be stored in it.

The search for the higher consciousness in man never was and is not a new one, for many have trodden this Path before us. Here I must warn you before a misunderstanding arises. If, in these pages you read much criticism of the mind, it is not directed against the use or even development of this power. Quite the opposite ! No spiritually eminent being was, or is weak-minded. Rather their mental abilities are astonishing and by far transcend all the scholars of their time. Read, for example, the sayings and answers of Christ, the Galilean carpenter, and try to correct or even improve on them ! Try to give your own answers to the questions put to Him by the very clever intellectuals and scholars of His epoch, without falling into one or another extreme, thereby leaving a weak point for the next attack. Usually, we do not appreciate the wisdom behind the sermons of the Great Teacher, and at the same time, we have nothing better to say or which can even be considered as wise. 'He that is without sin among you, let him first cast a stone at her.' 'Render therefore to Caesar the things that are Caesar's : and to God the things that are God's.' These, of course, are only two examples.

The main difference which divides an occultist from an official scientist is in his conception of the same power, that is, the *mind*. While the *first one* considers the mind to be his *servant*, and educates, broadens and develops it just for better service without ever losing his position as *master*, the *second* does not know of this division and usually identifies himself with that which should be his servant, but not master.

The *first*, if he is sufficiently developed, can say to his mental apparatus '*stop* until I tell you to do what I want', and he is able to enforce the execution of this order. For the *second* such a proceeding seems to be cumbersome and useless.

I leave it to the student himself to gather the consequences and form his own opinion in the matter.

*　　*　　*　　*

To return to the *direct means* which may bring us the Superconscious as if ready on a plate, it must be stated that such do not exist at all, just like the 'elixir of life' which is supposed to give unlimited physical existence. This should be well understood. All that can be done is to advise you about the inner processes which must be developed, as they have led other seekers to Samadhi, and can do the same for you. It is so strange, that in the realm which is the closest to every human being—his dearest possession, his *life*, devoid of the phantom of death—men forget the old and proved methods of official learning. Not for any price can you get a doctorate as if on a plate, but only by spending a certain number of years on serious study and practical work. If you get a fake diploma in engineering, it will be discovered at the first test when, for example, you try to build a modern bridge, without being a real engineer. The first technician will unmask you. It is exactly the same with spiritual knowledge, and how could it be otherwise? But so many people believe that they can embrace Wisdom merely by reading some books or instructions, even if the authors are really competent writers on occult philosophy.

The bulk of realizable work on the Path belongs to the individual experience of the aspirant, according to the lines he takes as his guides. Without our own effort the Path and the *aim* cannot be reached. Nobody can eat our food for us.

There are a few 'exceptions' (only apparent, of course) and they are very rare. There is the case of a man who, through the grace of a powerful Master was allowed to experience Samadhi *once* in its lower form, like an ecstasy, even despite his lack of the necessary training and former experience.

As a result he wrote a book, which afterwards led many of those who were ready to approach the Master. But inspiration, if not followed by adequate spiritual work and progress, cannot endure for ever and finally loses its power and becomes dissolved in everyday life.

Often the Master uses men as His tools to help bring about the fulfilment of His mission in this troubled world, and this is another invaluable opportunity for such people to progress rapidly, if they care enough about it.

Now we will return to the question of individual attainment, for which you are supposedly studying this work. At this point, when eighteen chapters of explanation, preliminaries and techniques lie behind you, your meditations should bring you the first glimpse of the new consciousness, manifesting itself firstly through the momentary flashes of *Light* in you. It is extremely hard to indicate exactly what the aspirant expects, when he sees the early rays of the great *Rising Sun* in himself. All that can be said is limited to comparisons: for what else do we have in our language of the mind? It operates solely with categories already *known*, if not by ourselves, then by others. The eternal, universal speech of the Absolute Consciousness (Samadhi) has no alphabet. The rays of its *sun* are imperceptible to the eyes of the flesh. Therefore the difficulty is immense, and the most strenuous efforts to convey the highest things are always inadequate, when compared with the actual *experience*. That is why Eastern Teachers speak so much about the ways to, and the necessity of, reaching Samadhi (Maharshi repeated : *Samadhi alone can reveal the truth*), but less about the *State* itself. They are very cautious in telling us more about the nature of that State. In the past Sri Sankaracharya was perhaps the ablest of them, as he gives some *positive* descriptions of certain states of consciousness attainable through Samadhi. Two of them have been given at the beginning of this chapter. Some others, equally inspiring may be quoted here :

'Realize that thou are "That"—*Brahman* which alone shines, which is beyond the Logos, all-pervading, uniform, truth, consciousness, bliss, having no end, indestructible. (Verse 264)

'When the mind, matured by ceaseless discipline of this kind, becomes merged in Brahman, then Samadhi, devoid of all forms . . . , becomes of itself the producer of the realization of non-dual bliss. (Verse 363)

'O thou, discriminating man ! Know renunciation and spiritual knowledge to be the two wings of the embodied ego. By nothing other than these two can ascent to the top of the creeper of nectar called liberation be accomplished.' (Verse 375)

But Samadhi does not come only to a seeker sitting in his lotus asana under a tree, which protects him from the merciless sun of India. As the Maharshi told us concerning Attainment, there is no difference whether a man is in a London flat, or in a solitary jungle retreat. Moreover, the Master added that *no change* of outer life will be of any help, because it is the *mind* of the seeker which has to be transformed, dominated and then transcended (in Samadhi), and *not the labels*, which one likes to attach to oneself, such as hermit, monk, yogi, and so on, instead of the inner evolutionary processes. So, if the problem of Attainment arises in you, it is virtually immaterial where you are and to which race or nationality you belong. Your ripeness is the deciding factor.

If you take this natural process of your spiritual ripening in your own hands, it will be accelerated and come nearer to you with every step ahead which you take on the thorny Path.

We know that, in this matter, no social or any other worldly position is of any actual importance. Those who have succeeded are generally unknown to the world, except for a few in history, who had a definite mission to serve humanity, to form a new religion, and so on, because they never speak about themselves.

Those who boast or advertise their 'Samadhi' are only deceivers, who have no idea about that sublime State, merely quoting from a few scriptures which they have never even properly understood.

This is because Samadhi necessitates such changes in human consciousness, that it would be impossible for a successful adept to retain even the slightest remnants of egoism and pride, which could induce him to speak about himself.

The Master Maharshi, although on the summit of all possible attainment, was never heard—throughout his long life—to speak about himself in any form. Even the personal pronoun *I* occurs only a few times in the translation of his answers to questioners. Moreover, although being a genuine Master-Guru, he never acknowledged this fact. Possessing the highest perennial Samadhi (Sahaja), he never mentioned it. And this is the case with all who really *know*.

The time when the aspirant will perceive the first rays of Samadhi's *sun* is unpredictable. Our investigations and experiments in this matter all seem to be negative. Here is meant, that the outer conditions, which can be noted by us, apparently have no influence on spiritual manifestations. Logically, moments of enlightenment should follow successful periods of meditation, but it is not so, and that a good state of health and nerves may promote it, is also not sufficiently confirmed to be quoted. Sometimes, when your body is definitely feeling low *It* happens!

Evidently, inner ripeness is beyond all the likely conditions in which we can occasionally find ourselves. I am comparing the first manifestations of Samadhi in human consciousness with the *Sunrise*. This is because they are just like an arising, transcendental, all penetrating Light in a man. This *Light* cannot be perceived with the eyes or by any of the other senses. Often when the eyelids are closed and the impact of the outer world thereby reduced, the phenomenon becomes stronger and lasts longer. Personally, I think that it is so great, that every physical reaction at that time is as if obliterated. If you are in the presence of other people, you will be aware of .the circumstances as usual, but as if looking from a far-off point of view, not in space, but in your consciousness. This aloofness brings full peace, although everything remains as it was.

There are no visions or other abnormal apparitions. And this is the *guarantee* that this state is not any mental delusion or ecstasy. Everything which was visible remains as such, but only the *point of view* of the seer is transformed on to a higher and brighter plane. The lucidity of this moment of Light is supreme. The person experiencing it knows, that if he could call himself 'homo sapiens' at any time, it is only *now*, in these minutes of intense happiness and wisdom. The term 'happiness' needs little explanation. One is simply filled with bliss which comes directly from the *Sun of Samadhi* rising in one. Then one is beyond all speech, so that the clothing of the experience in the language of mind only comes later, when all is over, but the mind still remains as if in bright twilight, after the Sunset of the Superconsciousness, and before the night of Jagrat (normal waking state) envelops everything again.

Physical movements are not yet hindered, as is the case in full Kevala Nirvikalpa, which can last for hours. Here one can still rise from sitting and walk, but speech comes with difficulty and only on the simplest of themes, which affect only the automatic activities of the brain, like asking for or showing a ticket, paying of money, crossing a street, and so on. No mental work beyond such simple patterns is possible, unless you stop the moments of enlightenment by breaking them because of thinking. But everything in us opposes such an action, and only the mute desire remains—to enjoy the Light for as long as possible. This desire, if it can be so termed, does not disturb the *Peace* inherent in the Sunrise. It seems that then man is simply beyond all expectations, anxieties and strivings, *and knows that everything is as it should be*. This last sentence, although not revealing even a fraction of the whole depth of this knowledge, nevertheless can be considered as being closest to the reality of the experience.

Another conception given by a friend who also saw the *Rising Sun* in his heart (as he called this spiritual flight) was that of a crystal clear, all penetrating immaterial light, like an unweighable liquid in which his individual consciousness was melted away to become united with this illimitable ocean of the *All*. Also the physical world did not completely disappear, for its nearest fragments were still perceptible, but as if in a mirror, reflecting far-off pictures.

In any case, the words of the Master Maharshi which tell us that in such a state there cannot be any thoughts, but only the pure *I-Self* consciousness, are fully confirmed by all those who *know*.

There is no sadness or grief in us when we return to the shadow of everyday life, for we preserve for ever the wisdom of our indestructible spiritual essence, which is beyond all the illusory pictures of the visible and tangible worlds. But the mightiest factor is the appearance in us of the pure *Hope* which tells us in the language of the Silence that our final destiny is just that *bliss*, a few faint fragments of which we had experienced a while before. This *Hope* finds its true realization in the next step, when, from the actual *spontaneous* manifestation of the *Rising Sun*, we begin to merge into the *Orb of Full Light* (Kevala Nirvikalpa Samadhi), as a result of calculated and successful efforts. You will be told about this in the last section of this book—Part IV.

After having experienced what it has been attempted to describe above, we begin to realize that the main cause why we cannot yet remain for ever in the *Light* lies only in ourselves and nowhere else.

The power which compels us to 'return' back into the Jagrat state is our inability to persist in the silent concentration which is the condition of the Sunrise. We see, that as soon as we fully realize this concentration (so far, only by chance), then we become desireless, without any 'spirit of expectation' (that great foe of inner peace), then the *reward* invariably comes. I have, apart from this, a firm conviction that the spiritual Master, who is invisibly watching the aspirant, may exercise his powers, even without any knowledge on the pupil's part, and mysteriously helps him to overcome—albeit for a short time—the main obstacles, apparently creating in him the inner attitude, which allows him to perceive the first dawn of the Light.

The aspirant may be utterly unconscious of this fact of invisible assistance, but the Great Beings do not care whether or not their actions are recognized. I think that even a modern saint (like Dr Albert Schweitzer) does not care whether a worm he saves on a pathway is aware of who spared its life. The difference between those few spiritual giants whose duty it is to assist us, who are erring and seeking Light through the darkness of this epoch, and average men, must be far greater than that between the worm and its human protector.

Why did I mention this? In order to make it clear to you that help is granted *only to those, who themselves try to assist their neighbours*. The Master as depicted above will not help a soulless egoist or those crawling after 'knowledge' for their own purposes. The Great Teacher unmistakably told us: 'Amen I say to you, as long as you did it not to one of these least, neither did you do it to me.' The Sun is always shining on the spiritual horizon, but average eyes do not see It, for they are looking only downwards on their perishable aims and businesses, in their flash of earthly existence.

A look, even only momentarily, at the *above* is the broadening of our usually narrow horizon of ego-existence. Do not delude yourself, that you can reach the point of spiritual enlightenment (we may call it Samadhi) by sitting in your study with innumerable books at your disposal, or merged in intellectual speculations and theories. All of them will die along with your body and its brain. From the point of view of Realization even a humble devotee, who prays to and bows before *That* which is his highest accessible conception of the Supreme, stands much higher and is more eligible for attention from a Master, than a cold egoist, who thinks that he collects wisdom from the printed or written thoughts and mental deliberations of other men, who did not, and do not know Truth, but only guess at It. You can read all Scriptures, the Bible and so on, right through, but if you do not perform what they command, your time is wasted. Here is meant the lack of spiritual effort usually manifesting itself in a selfless, inspired prayer, directed to the *Source* of all Wisdom. An eminent Indian scholar and Vedantist, the author of the famous '*Maha Yoga*' says rightly when he points out that 'the Vedas, and so on are only words and little more'. The letter alone is dead. St Paul the Apostle taught us, that even such a power as one of the three cardinal Christian virtues—*Faith* is dead if it is not accompanied by deeds.

* * * *

Three further meditations belonging to this chapter now lie before us. But a résumé would be desirable for this chapter, before we return to the meditations. The concluding statement is:

The higher states of consciousness are conditioned by (1) the high moral standards and (2) suppression of egoism, quite apart from (3) exercises, meditations and other techniques. The latter (3) will be of no use if they are not accompanied by (1) and (2) .

Verse 14: *Now there is nothing which can affect me any more.*
What does usually affect us and from where do these influences come? Which level of our consciousness do they affect? These questions, which have rightly occurred to us, should be answered, before we can state that they are not valid for us. We can be affected only in the realm of our three material planes of existence—physical, astral and mental. Refusal to yield to any physical influence means that nothing which happens to our body should affect our deepest *Core* —our *Self*. For untrained people it is easier to say than to realize. But we have many examples even from history, that some men were indifferent to the sufferings and death of their bodies. And not all of them were saints, enraptured by religious and spiritual ideas. Some were simply strong, courageous men who defied death because, in themselves, they found something stronger than the perishable body undergoing destruction. Therefore, there cannot be any question that he who strives for the highest, should be defenceless in the lowest. For our purposes immunity from the physical compulsion which affects our deepest consciousness, is one of the conditions of Attainment. It

can be obtained, if we strike with our main weapon at the present time, that is, meditation, against the old lie, so deeply rooted in incarnate humanity (a) *I am the body* or (b) *everything which happens to my body affects myself.*

Hence meditations must be directed against such mental formulas, and the best would be Verse 1 used in this book, serving as a firm and logical rejection of (a) and (b). The same will work with the astral and mental realms.

Emotions must be overcome and forbidden to trouble you, at first, during the time of your inner work (exercises), and later in general. There cannot be any talk about Samadhi when the aspirant suffers emotional disturbances, no matter of what kind. We know, from the description of the first rays of the invisible *Sun*, when it can rise in us and what it brings with it. So here also should be no doubt about the mental world, just as it was with the astral. In Samadhi *there are no thoughts but only I*, so if the aspirant did not secure himself against any mental intruders (thoughts) he cannot hope to obtain something, which comes only when all mental vortexes are extinguished, until they 'no longer affect' him. Again the hidden key to success is as before: *your lack of interest* (curiosity) *in lower things.* You may try as hard as you can to eliminate mentally, logically and in every other possible way the undesirable elements from your consciousness, using the best techniques known for that purpose, but if, in your deepest recesses, you have not conquered that secret and still alive *interest* in these things, they will finally erupt, on to the surface of your consciousness, as steam from under the lid of a boiler, and so destroy your meditation. This is the foremost practical initiation for solving the hard problem of astral and mental control of all aspirants on all genuine Paths.

Verse 15: *I am free from all names and forms.*

If the average man is asked the question: who he is?, the so-called natural answer will be, in the best of cases, *I am a man.* Under this term can be understood the man's body, plus the invisible elements which we call his emotional and mental worlds. With such ideas you can live your incarnation, while dreaming about the higher conceptions. *Samadhi is the ultimate negation of everything relative and temporal.* That is why it is so difficult, in fact rather impossible, to convey in speech or in any other form of mental communication, for it belongs to the realm of *That* which is absolute, unconditioned by anything, inaccessible to any influence, unchangeable by any factors, beyond time and all kinds of space. So nothing from the three-plane human has any access to Samadhi. Everything must be left before the *Great Gate*, if I may be allowed to use this symbol.

And those who have lived Samadhi know that they existed (and do exist) in *full*, even without these three elements which seemingly constitute every human being. But in Samadhi, man as we used to know him, does *not* exist. That is why the Lord Buddha rejected the idea of 'soul'; as do Advaita-Vedanta, Zen, and the genuine Western Initiatory Schools of Hermetic Tradition (their conception being *Ain-Soph*, the Unattainable, the Unknown).

In the Christian Tradition, now much obscured for laymen, we can still find similar ideas ('the material dies, but the spiritual arises' dogma).

Once when the Sage Maharshi spoke about himself, he said, that in truth he had no name at all. At the time few realized what he meant, and continued to address him as before.

To the foregoing description of the *Rising Sun* it may be added, that in this state 'namelessness and formlessness' are realized in full, being attributes of Samadhi. It is hoped, that after all that has been said about Verse 15, meditation about it may be made easier, and the student will realize, at least theoretically, what brings the Superconsciousness and what elements in himself should be abandoned before the threshold of full Samadhi.

At that time that which we call 'man' is *non-existent*, for then all becomes Silence, the Peace and Bliss of the eternally free Being.

Chapter XX

Discovery and Resurrection of the Eternal Principle in Man

Verse 415: 'Having approached the Logos which is eternal, pure knowledge and bliss, abandon this *upadhi* (the body) which is impure. Then it is not to be thought of again, the recollection of what is vomited is only calculated to disgust.'

Verse 416: 'The great wise man having burnt all this down to the roots in the fire of the eternal self, which is the non-dual Brahman in essence, remains in the Logos, which is eternal, pure knowledge and bliss.'

ALL that has been told in the previous chapters, as well as everything that has been written in occult and mystical books and treatises in any period, can be summarized as efforts in the direction of the practical and individual discovery of that which really is *Life* and the portion of it incarnate in man.

Reducing the whole problem to the part of it which is closest to us, we will call it—*the Eternal Principle in Man*. This is the broadest and hence most abstract conception, independent of the many specific terms and definitions, used in religions, philosophy and occultism. In order to make it more palatable for your mind, the following explanations may be used to describe the Eternal Principle in Man.

It is that which *exists* (in the meaning as given in Chapter XVII), lives, and manifests itself in a multiplicity of ways, so that we may observe and experience them. A keen student might add, that that is just what is used in this work as 'consciousness', and he will not be far from the truth. Awareness will be a necessary attribute of that Principle, but not of the kind you may have when sun-bathing, walking or dining, and so on. We will soon see why.

What is eternal always exists and manifests itself under any conditions. What does not possess this attribute of continuity, cannot belong to our *Principle* in question. When applied to ourselves, it would mean that an average, 'normal' human being is not endowed with this *Principle*, as his awareness (a function of the consciousness) has many interruptions, as in sleep, swoon, hypnotic states, and so on. This explains the famous saying of Krishnamurti: 'Your *I* does not exist even now!' He evidently spoke about that small, temporal and perishable *I* which people unfortunately consider to be themselves. From our point of view such incomplete awareness is rather similar to non-existence than to true existence. To those unacquainted with the practical possibility of uninterrupted consciousness (that is, always functioning without cessation in the state of death, as well as of sleep), these conceptions will remain unreal, and this is quite understandable, so there is no reason to delve into it any more; especially so as Christ Himself called such people 'dead'.

In modern occultism (see *The Tarot*) this state is labelled as the 'sleep of ignorance'. P. D. Ouspensky, in his later years, when he managed to set himself free from the ominous influence of Gurdjieff, referred to it as 'the war against deadly sleep'. Rom Landau, the author of a very important book (among others)—*God is My Adventure*, which contains much keen reporting, attended the lectures of Ouspensky in London in the early thirties, and was appreciative of the uncompromising attitude of this Russian intellectual and mystic.

So, we can define the average state of human consciousness as a not-yet-awakened one. Then the efforts directed to raising our consciousness to the higher and wider levels can easily be termed as leading to the new, real 'waking' state, which, in occult philosophy is called Samadhi or Superconsciousness. Therefore, the discovery of Samadhi in ourselves is equal to the realization of the *Eternal Principle* in us.

The student is advised to meditate about the contents of this part of the present chapter before he starts on its continuation.

*   *   *   *

In the hope that this has been done, we may now proceed to the actual manifestation of this *Priciple* in man. On this level all labels like 'soul', Spirit, Atman, and so on, are better temporarily forgotten, for now we seek the bare response in us to the definition of that *Principle*. It will be no other formula than *I am*. There is nothing and cannot be anything apart from and beyond It. *I am* is the name of every human being: the magic name possessing the illimitable *power* of Realization. It is also the answer to the mysterious and so often misunderstood Vichara, given to us by the great Rishi Ramana, as the universal means for finding the highest in man.

I am is therefore the *only* real speech of man, *I am* whispers the unity of the whole of humanity. I say 'whispers' for only a few are able to hear this still dim voice of Truth in humanity and realize its *Oneness*.

What can the whole immense universe say? Anything apart from *I am* would inevitably spoil the answer. This universe is only unreal because there is no other as it *is*, therefore there *is* nothing to oppose and to create again the destructive binary, as in lower worlds, of the illusory visions which constitute Maya.

Finally, the *Highest Principle Itself* (which some like to call 'God') has nothing to reveal beyond that magnificent biblical development of the same mystical formula : '*I am that I am*.' Meditate about this before you go any further.

*   *   *   *

In defining the indescribable state of Samadhi, Sri Maharshi told us, that its chief characteristic is the presence of the sole 'feeling'—*I am* and nothing more, with no thoughts or other outer activity of the consciousness.

Finally, if we are initiated into its use, the *I am* truth is our supreme weapon against all troubles on all three planes. This means, that we then have to 'remember' our high origin, as rays of the *Central Light* of the *Absolute Consciousness* reflected in us and broken up by passing through the manifested world, just as a prism breaks up the primordial *white* light into several separate colours. This is a metaphysical explanation of the conceptions of 'variety' and 'multiplicity' in the broadest sense. It was used by the great Rishi Ramana, when he tried to convey to his questioners the idea of the relationship of God and His universe, including human beings.

If this phenomenon of the prism is applied to the *Central* non-disintegrated *Consciousness*, then we have (in the human world) different manifestations in the form of different men. *As above so below*, but this condition does not continue indefinitely. The law of evolution causes the *Differentiated* to gravitate again to the primary *Oneness*. In other words, Isis collects together the strewn parts of Osiris's body, according to the ancient, traditional Egyptian interpretation of that law. It was a part of their final initiation.

Here also lies the mystery of Superconsciousness. From individual fragments of it, in the not yet reintegrated beings (like ourselves), the Path leads to the *unbroken* Unity, reflected in the primordial *White Light*. Properly speaking, the title of this chapter could just as well be the '*Rediscovery* of the Eternal Principle in man', for the essential Oneness was, is and will be for ever, for it is eternal, being only temporarily veiled by a merging into the separate mortal existence.

The Path is just a way to the realization of this great Principle. Do not think that all this is only theory for those who are initiated into the Essence of the Principle. For them it is as real as anything which you see around you at this moment. It is worth mentioning that the foremost manifestation of the illusion of separateness (that is, personality and then—individuality) is *egoism*, and the combating and destruction of this ancient arch-enemy, this evil ghost which deceives humanity as the biblical serpent tempted and deceived Eve, is the cardinal aim of every spiritual (that is, reintegrating) movement. All spiritual giants, whom we call great Saints, yogis, and Rishis, that is, those who realize the Oneness long before the rest of humanity, have left as the first commandment for us, who try to follow those leaders: *the destruction of the primordial sin* (as the Maharshi termed it), which is *belief in being separate and egoism*.

We cannot close our eyes to the sad fact, that in the present epoch (Kali-Yuga according to the Hindus), the *Eternal Principle* is being discovered only by a few forerunners, the mass of men still remaining deep in the swamp of separateness-egoism. Apart from having separate bodies (physical and the rest) we deepen all this further by creating our own fences which we call: family egoism, class egoism and national egoism. On its present level, humanity is convinced that this deepening of separation is necessary for its own happiness, which, unfortunately, cannot and *is not found* in such a way.

There is another simile: in a hive, worker bees divide the honey between separate honeycombs; but when the time comes for it to be collected, it is pressed out and the separating combs removed, until a uniform mass of honey is ready.

This is the 'harvest' of which Christ often spoke as being the ultimate aim and end of every life.

In Samadhi the Oneness is *realized* in full. When we reach this state, we rediscover the *One Truth* for ever. Then there are no more questions, ignorance or doubts. But, how many are ripe enough to make this final discovery?

*   *   *   *

From the point of view of Oneness the 'normal' state of consciousness of the average egoist, who believes in his 'separate' existence, is comparable to spiritual death. The great Teacher once said: 'Let the dead bury their dead.' Therefore, the attainment of Unity in Samadhi (it cannot be realized otherwise) is similar to resurrection. The two basic principles, the *dawn* (or birth) in us of the One Central Consciousness and the final resurrection to the eternal life beyond all forms and separation can be found in a veiled form in all the great religions of this planet. The keen student may also discern them in ancient mythology. We will mention here only the Christian Christmas and Easter, which are very transparent symbols for the drama of evolution.

These are the esoteric and occult teachings, reflected in denominations. But we have to have our own experimental knowledge and proofs of them. And these you will find in Samadhi, when you reach it. You will find that state akin to a glorious resurrection, to realization of the Absolute Oneness and in this lies the inexpressible and incomparable bliss of the Superconsciousness.

Verse 16: *I have forgotten the dream of earth.*

After what we have just read, this meditation will not present any difficulties in its understanding and practice. After having rediscovered the Truth (another name for the Eternal Principle) and being resuscitated in the miracle of spiritual resurrection, who would even remember the shadows of his former wanderings through the earthly (or other) incarnations? Who would like to descend into a dark, dank cellar after bathing in the life-giving rays of the Sun? One simply tries to forget the former darkness, as is anticipated in Verse 16 of our meditation for this chapter.

In Samadhi we know who we are, and although this spiritual knowledge cannot be shaped into the language of mind, there is one truth, which will invariably be brought back from Samadhi: *I have nothing in common with that fleshly shell left somewhere on the earth.*

Spiritual consciousness does not leave any room for the body, created from dust and returning to it. Is all this possible? It is, because we have innumerable proofs and examples given by men, who showed true contempt for and superiority over their fleshly cases. The best test of whether a man identifies himself with his body or is able to transcend it, is his death. Saints and martyrs openly preferred to abandon their material shells in order to live in spirit. The same has been done by men who have died for their ideas or sacrificed themselves for others. None of these would have done so, if they had no intuitional, even some direct, knowledge about the prevailing of Spirit over matter. But not all who have showed their readiness to die have been good examples for our present theme. Men do not commit suicide because they possess some higher knowledge, but only because of extreme despair, in order to flee from sufferings which, to them, as they believe, are worse than death. Such people are seeking annihilation, but not any superior life, about which they do not know anything.

Therefore we should discriminate carefully when drawing our

conclusions. There are also some kinds of 'compulsory courage' in the face of death, mainly created by certain special circumstances, such as mass hypnosis on the battlefield, plus hysteria. A man who was well known for his great courage and fearlessness. when facing death in battle said, that: 'everyone has fear, the only difference being that the courageous person does not show it.' A circumstantial (relative) truth undoubtedly lies in this statement.

A classical and evergreen example of man's detachment from his body and of the certainty of the prevailing of Spirit over the mortal form is given to us in the accounts by Plato (see the *Crito*) of Socrates' end. The sublime sincerity, simplicity and greatness of this sage in his last hours make his death a luminous and encouraging example of the heights to which the human spirit is able to raise itself. Many sensible people, when reading the famous dialogue *Crito*, have expressed the desire to behave themselves like Socrates in their last hours.

The Great Rishi Ramana also taught us that the only evil in man can be his deeds, feelings and thoughts, but *not the man himself* (that is, his true Self-Atman), who is strong and good.

This gives us great hope. Otherwise, this statement is in perfect accord with logic and occult tradition as well. The supreme quality in man, which is also proof of his spirituality (Realization of the true being—*Self*) is his pure altruism, that is complete lack of egoism. The latter is the child of the *Body am I* belief. But one can actually test for oneself, that this spiritual *Core* exists in us, and manifests itself even in not so highly developed individuals.

It is the complete selflessness of this cardinal virtue, which inevitably attracts everyone and compels admiration. Otherwise why have some modern representatives of this divine virtue exercised such a strong attraction for so many human hearts? I will mention only two of these great souls, of quite different races, traditions, religions and countries, but possessing the same brilliant light, manifested as perfect altruism and lack of usual human weaknesses. When we read the enthusiastic and loving accounts of those who contacted St Jean de Vianney of Ars (France) or Ramana Marharshi of India, we may understand what powerful magnets are those great Sons of Humanity, in whose lives and example lies the hope of erring mankind, at least the hope of its best representatives.

Everyone knows that we are living in a truly critical period for incarnate humanity. We know that everything which has a beginning must also have an end. Mankind as one of the materialized manifestations of the *Unique Life* cannot be an exception to that axiom. When the outer forms become unsuitable and conditions created by and for them offer no opportunity for the evolution of the sparks of consciousness enclosed in them, general dissolution must come in due time. This is a great and impenetrable mystery for the human mind, and it cannot be operated by intellect. When a Great Teacher spoke about this inevitable event of a planetary end, the question about time was put to Him by His disciples. The Master only emphasized the impossibility of such an answer in terms of human speech, when He told them, that: 'But of that day or hour no man knoweth, neither the angels in heaven, nor the Son, but the Father.'

The Father is the unmanifested, Absolute-Spirit, whom 'nobody but the Son knows' (the pure and direct manifestation of the Supreme Unknowable). In this quality, being *One* with the Father the Great Teacher *knew*, but in His quality as incarnate Man, He could not unveil what is beyond the language of the mind, the only one accessible to us.

And even if it were possible, there would be no need or use for such a terrible prophecy. For those who are more ripe are not interested or frightened to learn, that the end of their incarnations is close. And those of the far less advanced majority simply would not believe in any prediction, just as they did not ages before, until it becomes truly materialized, and then everything is too late and meaningless.

Mankind now stands before two paths, two possibilities. One is a powerful evolutionary step ahead, away from the present bypaths, which are based on unconditional egoism, personal as well as national, the latter being no less evil than the former. The other is the bearing of the consequences of the temporary, unsuccessful evolutionary epoch, which means a general dissolution of this planet, which is often referred to as 'the end of the world', although, of course, it is not so, but merely a change of decor on the same eternal screen of Life.

The attentive student will certainly realize that all this has no meaning for the *Eternal Principle* in him, which in reality is beyond any forms, time and space. When in Samadhi man is not affected by any outer changes around him.

A practical experience can be recommended, which will be of great profit for every aspirant on the Path. Regularly dedicate some time to thinking, in full inner peace, of yourself as a non-material being, living only by feeling and thought, but *not* by any bodily functions. This, of course, will not be any high spiritual flight, but only a separation from the densest body. Imagine and try to believe, that you, at that moment, *do not need any physical things and are despising all of them*. Be satisfied with your mental processes, looking down, as if from a high mountain, on the physical person which you are in the visible world. This is a kind of meditation, and the key to its realization is, as with every meditation, the start of the point of *silence* in the brain. From this, begin to 'float' in the mental ocean, not as an occupant of a rudderless boat, but as a conscious sailor, who knows where he wants to travel. For example, think about other worlds in other galaxies. This has been proved to produce a considerable degree of liberation from the narrow, ego-brain thinking. You may also meditate about some elevated ideas, borrowed from the leading minds of humanity, and so on.

If steadfastly performed, this exercise will make your tight bonds with the bodily functions less compelling and binding. You may then gradually develop the habit of being more 'ethereal' at certain times, and the possibility of existence apart from the body and its occupations may dawn in you.

When a final abandonment of the dense form is unavoidable, why not try some preparation for the fact, in order to secure more peace and certainty at the critical hour?

What should be well grasped, is that in this exercise your 'normal' (as they are usually called) human interests must be obliterated. This is the whole secret. For that time forget your worries, strivings, social and personal ties with the surrounding human world and its attachments. Do not think about yourself as that biped being, with many labels, which stick only to the body: name, sex, position, titles, and so on. Be *free* from all of them, even for that short time of meditation, and you will find that the reward is truly great for those who are able to raise their heads over the edge of the limited world around them.

Chapter XXI

The Last Warnings on the Path

Verse 163: 'O you of deluded judgment, abandon the opinion that the self consists in the mass of skin, flesh, fat bone, and filth; know that the real self is the all-pervading, changeless *atman* and so obtain peace.'

WHEN the aspirant has lived his *first moments of enlightenment,* as is presumed in Chapter XIX, the next step will come as the development of a controlled ability to enter into Samadhi for longer periods. At first it is usually for some minutes, which gradually extend into a couple of hours. This has been observed and the rule deduced from it. But different lengths of time can elapse between the first rays of the Rising Sun of Samadhi in the heart of the aspirant, and the merging with full consciousness in Kevala Nirvikalpa. These can vary from weeks (very rare cases) to whole incarnations. There are limits, but practically it may be said that there are years of effort between the two aforementioned phases of development.

All depends upon the ripeness and eagerness of the disciple, and the same can be said concerning the necessary help of an Older Brother, called Master or Guru, who does not always take human form. In practice the Guru helps us 'from inside' and this is only logical. What we need is the *spiritual* impulse, so why expect a physical appearance for such a purpose? Man is *consciousness,* but not his shells, which put him into sensory contact with the environment of a relatively short period of descent into dense matter. The *Core* is all, and for It the Master exercises his *spiritual* powers, not otherwise.

Some warnings should now be given, as they can save you much toil and disappointment, if grave errors are committed on the Path.

Principally, this touches on the very important period of 'in between', as was said previously, that is, during the time from the first rays of the Superconsciousness until the first voluntary and prolonged experience of Kevala Samadhi. Because, when it is reached, much less probability of failure exists, as the *Full Light* is a thing which cannot be easily forgotten for the temptations and false pleasures of Maya.

163

Firstly, do not allow yourself to be over enthusiastic, immediately expecting some miraculous development in you. You are still standing with your feet firmly on the earth, and sometimes only your head looks into the higher regions. Do not forget this! Most certainly such a wonder will not happen, and all the wisdom will not come with the *Rising Sun*, but much later.

Exceptions, which I have to mention, are too rare and require the physical presence of a Guru, who is the Teacher for the epoch in which you live on this planet. But this is a very slight chance, as you know from the previous statements (see Part IV of *Concentration*).

Therefore, it would be reasonable to rest assured, that there cannot be any mistake in our destiny (karma) for the present incarnation, and that the inner development follows gradually, according to the disciple's efforts and karmic conditions. Here endurance is the foremost virtue.

The flashes of Light will appear at intervals, which may also take days or even years, and no one can predict them.

If you agree with all sincerity that the best which can be done is to wait patiently, persistently practising the meditations as recommended in this work, then you will be doing your best to promote the hidden progress. I say 'hidden', for you cannot control it until well advanced in Kevala Nirvikalpa. So taught the Master Maharshi, who brought into this world so much light about the Superconsciousness and its possible achievement by us.

The 'blessed moments' come unexpectedly, mostly just when you are not thinking about them, and therefore your mind is less penetrated by the vibrations which come from the outer world and its clichés. Again, you will note an important circumstance: the periods of the spontaneous flashes of Samadhi are longer, when you firmly guard your mind against all thoughts, and concentrate your physical sight on one (no matter which) point before you. There is no need, at this stage, to close the eyes; I even think this would not be desirable, as it might shorten the experience, which you want to last for as long as possible.

Some aspirants find that the slow repetition of a short mantra, well known to them, is a positive means for retaining the *Sun Rise* longer. So try to use the mental recitation of *Aum*, which has proved to be very effective, or even *I am*, approximately not more than six to ten times per minute, that is, slowly. Never allow the mind to be occupied with the feverish expectation of 'something which might still come'. *Nothing* more will come at this stage. Another warning: do not think, in your free time, about the fact that you are gaining some enlightenment. It would not be helpful. Be careful that no hidden pride arises in you just because you may be a little advanced beyond your fellow men. Pride will kill your spiritual flights, because it is a gross manifestation of the old, cruel and destructive foe called *egoism*, which Sri Sankara so wisely calls 'a terrible tiger'. Perhaps the next warning will be the most essential : do not dare to tell anyone about your experiences, unless you have a friend who is more advanced than yourself, but as it is very hard to establish this, the best course is complete silence. What good can come from your boasting before others? It will surely not bring them to the same point which you have possibly reached. Instead it is certain that the result will bring you a lot of bitterness. You might be subjected to much mockery, belittling, malicious gossip, suspicions of being an imposter and often, the hidden but acute jealousy from the side of those who are unable to experience states similar to those you have experienced.

Remember the words of Christ : '*Neither cast ye your pearls before swine. . . .*'

In this period of your development everything depends on yourself : your seriousness and earnest striving to advance, not only for your own sake, but simply because every man who forges ahead of the mass of humanity, pulls the whole a little way along with himself, although he can never see this fact. But so have taught all the Masters from the oldest Rishis and Saints to Sankaracharya and Maharshi. They know better.

'*Prepare, and be forwarned in time. If thou hast tried and failed, O dauntless fighter, yet lose not courage: fight on, and to the charge return again and yet again . . .*

Remember, thou that fightest for man's liberation, each failure is success, and each sincere attempt wins its reward in time. . . .'

(From *The Voice of the Silence, The Seven Portals.*)

Do not commit any extravagances. Do not suddenly change your way of life, so that others might notice it. Your karmic duties still remain as they were before, so do not forcibly break what, theoretically, you may consider as kinds of chains. When an over-enthusiastic, that is, unreasonable devotee came to the Master Maharshi and declared that he intended to abandon his wife and young children in order to become a sannyasin (hermit) near the Maharshi's Ashram, the latter did not support such a decision.

He firmly disapproved of such an intention, pointing out that there would be only a change of label of the same still imperfect and unsubdued personality and mind. True asceticism is an inner state, not an assumed position or title. And it can be practised in any conditions. When the experiences, which must be performed in worldly surroundings, are over and you have learned the necessary lessons of life in full, then karma itself will arrange other conditions for you, perhaps allowing you an anchorite's existence, in this or another incarnation.

And it will be a suitable one and at an appropriate time. The fact that Great Masters who have real missions for humanity are not burdened by any adverse karmas to obstruct their teachings is a further proof of the foregoing.

The foremost 'excuse' which weak-willed and ignorant individuals use in order to explain and justify their passivity in spiritual efforts, is just this 'lack of propitious conditions', which do not allow them to take steps towards the Path. As long as such an attitude persists, there will be no 'suitable conditions' in any future incarnations.

In this age it has been observed that apparently adverse karmic conditions and other difficulties in life can often be *positive* factors for creating in men the attitude of searching for higher values, than those of the cruel, material world. Suffering, being a payment for errors committed is also a kind of school, in which one learns to recognize the law of karmic retribution. That is why a proverb tells us, that those who have suffered much, also possess a greater understanding. It is in this spirit that every suffering must be accepted, and *not* with inner revolt or cursing of fate, for this will only bring new waves of disaster. So be aware of this warning as well.

If you let people know that you have had some spiritual experiences, you may thereby attract the attention of two categories of men to your activities. One type will try to exploit you materially by offering help for 'quick advancement to perfection', of course, for a suitable reward, more or less cleverly disguised—while another will want to accept you as their 'teacher' or even 'master', in order to have the same experiences. They might even offer you payment for such a service.

It can happen only when you have talked too much, as was warned elsewhere in this chapter. Of course, in such a case, you will have only one task: to get rid of both kinds of individuals and never give any further opportunity for anyone to bother you.

*   *   *   *

It was observed, that soon after the first enlightenment, the aspirant may undergo some attacks from the forces which try to prevent any extraordinary spiritual progress from the side of human beings. Unfortunately, such forces exist, and it would not be advisable for the writer to hide this fact. After what has already been explained in this connection in *Concentration* there remains little to add now.

Anyway, the opposition may be materialized in the form of strong temptations appearing just at the time when one wants to purify one's life. Some aspirants have been astonished at why the impure and violent currents have assaulted them, just at the time when they seemed to be leading a most balanced and clean life, subsequent to their enlightening experiences. There is a law in inner life, which allows temptations and sufferings to manifest in our karmas proportionally to our strength and endurance to support them. Nobody receives anything beyond his or her possibilities of resistance. When more difficulties appear, it is the sign that a man is able to pay more 'instalments' in order to purify his karma. Read the lives of the Saints and you will find how terrible were the experiences which they were compelled to endure (see a recently published book *Miser of Souls* by Margaret Trouncer, Hutchinson, of London).

The onus is on the student, whether he endures and stands firm, or —falls. This warning may be useful for those who may feel some discouragement on contacting the opposing forces at the beginning of their Path. Know that this is only natural and they have been sent to us in order to be overcome and conquered.

There is another kind of erroneous attitude, which might cancel all further progress in a careless aspirant and this is when he considers (usually subconsciously, because of lack of self-control) his spiritual endeavour as a savoury addition to his 'normal', that is physical life. You must realize that the Path and its Aim—the transfer of the consciousness from the three lower levels, belonging to the mortal world, into the heights of Samadhi—must receive *all priority from you and stand before everything else.*

The *whole man* is needed and not any 'part time layman' bungling with certain opportunities concerning things of the highest order.

You cannot lead the life a dandy or come home late from a nightclub or cabaret and then try your meditations. In such a case it would be only a loss of time and frustration of the expected reward. How can a man attain purity in Spirit, which is the first qualification for the attainment of the Superconsciousness, and at the same time, be impure physically, astrally and mentally? Nobody would expect a saint to be a gambler, a drunk or a weak-willed man, a prey of emotions and unable to control his mind.

Great help will be obtained on this point by reading of the lives of Saints, because we get a moral lift from the mysterious magnetism in such literature, which turns us from lower things to more lofty conceptions and decisions.

This is a well-proven fact, which can be tested and experienced by every earnest aspirant.

When St Seraphim of Sarov taught his monk-disciples how they might try to get spiritual enlightenment like himself, he always pointed out that the first condition is inner peace, born from non-attachment to worldly affairs and the extermination of all inner vanity, transforming this vice into the virtue of humility, which is the beginning of Wisdom. Such an attitude would also be helpful for the eradication of the main obstacle, that is, egoism in man. A different kind of injunction may be recommended for a person living in the twentieth century: *do not commit any nonsense in your life.* A new discrimination is needed and a steady insight sought for the development of the quality of right judgement in every case. These qualities and their creation have already been spoken about in preceding chapters.

Several methods are used in occultism for that purpose. One of the best is to put a question to ourselves before every action:

> *Is what I am about to do helpful and not opposite to my path? Would the Master praise or blame me for it? Is it just a wasting of my time?*

If you analyse your actions in such a way, you will not lose any period of your life for activities, which later will bring you only shame. This analysis is necessary until regular flashes of Samadhi appear, for then the potent influence of the Rising Sun will teach you better than any words can do.

Such are the final warnings about certain negative factors which may prevent you from attaining the *Orb of Full Light*, of which more is said in the next and final chapter of this book.

If some questions arise in you, which are *not* born from any mental (that is useless) curiosity, but from difficulty in understanding certain statements and conceptions connected with this work, the writer can be contacted for further explanation.

PART IV

Attainment

Chapter XXII

In the Orb of Full Light

Verse 483: 'The greatness of *parabrahman,* like an ocean completely filled with the nectar of realized bliss, can neither be described by speech nor conceived by mind, but can be enjoyed. Just as a hailstone falling into the sea becomes dissolved therein, so my mind becomes merged (even) in the least part of this (*parabrahman*). Now am I happy with spiritual bliss.'

Verse 484: 'Where is this world gone? By whom was it carried away? When did it disappear? A great wonder! That which was perceived but now exists no longer.'

Verse 486: 'Here (in the state) I neither see, nor hear, nor know anything. I am different from every other thing—the atman who is true bliss.'

THERE still remains one step, which is possible for successful aspirants, who have experienced the *Rising Sun.* This last step we call the entrance into the *Orb of Full Light.* Why? Because the state of *Kevala* Nirvikalpa Samadhi—which as you know, means *temporary, formless Superconsciousness* —is the highest one about which man can think and speak and experience while still living on this earth. In this state the former tool of cognition, the *mind,* is temporarily merged into the *Central Light* which is *All* that really exists. It is God, if you prefer this term: it is Spirit, Nirvana, the Kingdom of Heaven and everything else which men call the highest *Being-State* which is accessible to them.

This state does not persist for ever. Its manifestation is limited in time, as observed from the physical plane. For then the experiencer is living beyond all time and space. But, nevertheless he *returns.* This is the justification for the word 'Kevala'. And that is why I say that then mind is only 'merged' in the *Light,* while the term 'dissolved' belongs to the *Sahaja* Nirvikalpa Samadhi, that is, the perennial one. In this state, the mind is *not immersed,* but *dissolved,* that is, it *cannot* return to its former functions, as in an ordinary man. Sri Maharshi uses a stronger definition for this. He says, that in Sahaja the mind is *dead*, and cannot have any essential link with the consciousness of the man who has attained this *peak*. You should have a clear and firm realization of this.

No mortal man can ever speak about Sahaja Samadhi, for such a person can never experience it. It is the privilege of the fully reintegrated, perfect *men*, those rare jewels produced by evolution on this planet, or elsewhere. We call those few luminous Beings, who have appeared for our sakes—Perfect Masters, Great Teachers, Sons of God, all of which are synonymous.

Those who have raised their consciousness to Kevala, *know* that in that state it is impossible to perform any physical activities, for the first condition for merging in it is absolute passivity of the body, then entering into a state similar to catalepsy, because of the immobility and insensitivity of the physical shell of those who enter into this form of Samadhi. Often even the breath stops, however without causing any danger or ill effects for the body. This is a miracle, for official science tells us, that the cessation of breathing for more than a few minutes means death. But here the period of absence of respiration can be measured in hours.

Those who experience it can only say that for them it is another proof that Spirit can in fact dominate matter and its apparently immutable laws. We cannot give any other explanation, how it can be, that although no oxygen is introduced into the organism, and the pulse becomes as if non-existent, the process of decomposition does not start at all, as invariably happens when these two vital functions cease because of factors other than Samadhi.

And now comes the greatest mystery, which has never been solved except by a man of the Master's level. How is it possible to experience Samadhi (in its Sahaja form) continuously and at the same time be active in the physical body, to speak, eat, move, and so on, without lowering the consciousness for even a fraction of a second, to the level of mind?

Only those who have looked into the eyes of a true Master have no doubts about this wonder. They know that *it is so*, but that is all. No commentaries can be given, and therefore we will not return to this problem any more, as it would be useless. The building of theories and guessing is not a method which leads to Truth, but only temporary conceptions which ceaselessly change in our minds. We know that this is not compatible with the Path.

So the fact that Kevala will be our final aim and attainment (in so far as we still have to evolve, being as yet imperfect) remains as axiomatic for an earnest aspirant. He will not be concerned with what is beyond his reach.

It is believed in occult circles (as well as taught in the Eastern initiatory Scriptures), that the way from the 'normal' consciousness in man to the point where he reaches Kevala Samadhi, is incomparably shorter and less arduous than that from the Kevala to Sahaja. If you are on the Path, you know how difficult it is, and you will not force your imagination to build for you the inconceivable heights and labour necessary to reach them. We should always remain reasonable beings, rejecting all unwanted wandering of the mind.

So all we can speak about concerns the temporary flights into the realm of *Light* in Kevala Samadhi.

But here again arises an obstacle which seems impossible to overcome: the experiences of Samadhi are completely beyond any functions of the mind, which can only dictate descriptions using its language (that is, human speech).

Well, nobody has been, is, or will be able to reflect in his utterances the full Light and Bliss of pure Superconsciousness. If you think deeper about it, the right solution must come. If Samadhi is beyond any space, time, feelings and thoughts, and is itself *conditioned* by just the *absence* of these factors in your consciousness, how can you expect to hold water in a sieve, or to establish limits and frontiers for Infinity? Therefore, all that can be brought back from Samadhi has the same relation and reality (properly speaking, the *absence* of reality) to it, as the reflection of the sun in a jar of water. The image seemingly exists, and we can see it, but what has it in common with the magnificent life-giving star in our sky? Moreover, there can be as many reflections of the sun as there are jars or other means which will catch the image of the immensity on infinitesimally small surfaces. Add still the fact, that all the pictures and reflections of the sun do not, and cannot, affect the real object of perception, and it may help you to grasp the idea which is trying to be conveyed to you in these paragraphs.

There is one undeniable fact: everyone returning from Samadhi into his 'normal' state of consciousness, that is, that of the mind, experiences immense bliss and enlightenment. But the Master Maharshi told us, that all this is only a tiny reflection of the *Light* in the mind, and that it is often accompanied by different forms of ecstasy, tears, even singing and in the case of a few men, by dancing as if in a trance. But usually, and especially with intellectual men, these outer expressions of happiness do not take a visible form, remaining hidden in the man's *inner sanctuary*, which we know about from Chapter IX. The Master, who possesses Sahaja Samadhi, never gives any particulars, or tries to explain the full bliss of this state, and so the

Maharshi answered all his interrogators, who were curious to know the unknowable, by advising them to secure the Realization of the true *Self* for themselves, adding that then they would be able to know everything from their own experience, without which any words are of little help.

But we are all still human, until such time as we transcend our humanity in the glory of Mastership, and a long way lies before us.

So, perhaps, even these reflections, as imperfect as the image of the sun in a pool of water, may bring us some new ideas about the *Light* and its imperishable *Orb*.

While being conscious of everything that has just been said, and bowing to the dust before *Those* whose consciousness is for ever united with that *Light*—being that *Light Itself*—we will attempt to put into words, some reflections, brought from the *Orb*.

*   *   *   *

Verse 17 : *I am the all-penetrating Infinite Life. I am—I am All.*

This is the last and most transcendental meditation of this whole course. And it is the last preparation for the Kevala. How long should you practise it? The answer is clear : until it works, that is, until you are able to exchange your flashes of *Light* for deliberately arranged merging into the Superconsciousness for a longer time. No one else can do it instead of you, and it is *you* who decides about the success or failure.

A few explanations can be given again, which might facilitate just the inner tuning to this meditation.

Realize deeply in your mind, that *Life* is *Existence*, as was mentioned in former chapters. Existence thereby meaning the *Unchangeable, having no beginning nor end*. This depth can be reached. *Firstly*, because your ultimate human *Core* is just this *perpetual existence*, it is in you, and in vain will you seek after it elsewhere than in yourself. So all the trumps are in your own hands. Meditate about this for a while.

Secondly, because others have reached *It*, or *That*, and they have given testimony to this fact, they are the Masters.

This Existence, Life is beyond all and if something still exists, it must be in *It*, for otherwise it would be *apart* from *Life* and *Existence*, which means *non-existence*, a mirage, an absolute *zero*, or—nothingness. Such things cannot interest us, as they are nothing and disappear with the first ray of Wisdom directed at them. In the East they say that Maya vanishes like a mist before the Atman's Light.

The next step, is to identify yourself with that Absolute Life. It will be easy if you have learned by concentration, to merge your I into the Silence of *Self*, even for a very short time. Some people have a certain innate ability to merge in the peace of the Silence. They will better understand what I mean.

In spite of the apparent difficulty for many aspirants, connected with the transfer of the consciousness from the individual to the Whole, and thereby becoming that *All*, the thing is actually supremely simple. Perhaps just in this fact lies the difficulty, as for innumerable separate existences men acquired the strong habit of considering themselves as separate units, and the complexity of their minds, so different from the supreme *simplicity* of *Oneness*, is the foremost obstacle. These minds, instead of merging into their *Source*, as taught the Maharshi, try to pour out unnecessary (but somewhat burning for them) questions like: why, how, for which purpose, in which way, and so on, instead of *living the spiritual experience in full*, which fact alone can bring the final answer to *all the questions at once*. This is another mystery of Achievement, which awaits the successful aspirant at the end of his Path. So, all such questions are unnecessary and brakes to progress, as Wisdom is different from and superior to knowledge.

But, suppose that you reached the aim and obtained the wisdom of Oneness of Being in yourself. What happens then?

You are already deep in meditation, the outer world was long ago beyond the light of your consciousness. The great moment is close. You enter into your legitimate kingdom of *All*, of God, of Spirit: terms are without meaning in this degree of awareness. Now It Is! Like the flame of a candle extinguished by a mighty blow, the last vestiges of duality disappear. There is no more mind. Through the Silence, now becoming perfect in you, the Allness takes you into its power. There are no more forms, and there is no more death or change. Where is the world with all its complications of time, space and the manifestations of a separate existence? The dream is finished for ever. *I am* reigns supreme in all. This consciousness has no limits, and it is not seeking any movement. It reaches everywhere, but there is no such thing as *far* or *near*. There is no *I* or *Non-I*. Like an infinite ocean of purest crystal, the *I* extends into infinity, and is also concentrated on the non-material (because of its smallness) geometrical point. The impossible *in relativity* becomes *reality in Samadhi*.

The white ray, broken into different colours by the prism of the world, inserted in its way, is reintegrated in its primordial purity in the experiencing of this supreme state. There is no more action or reaction, for there is *no doer* in the infinity of Spirit. In the Bliss of the Allness, in the Perfection of the Primordial, non-disintegrated Consciousness there cannot be born anything like action, based purely on relativity.

There is no time, and no expectation or compulsion of change. But this is not peace or the silence of death, of non-existence! On the contrary, It is the essence of all Life, independent and unobstructed by anything, melted in Eternity, which is the final solution for everything.

Words are so poor, so powerless to render the true meaning of the Consciousness of the Future, at this present time.

As the mind has been evaporated in the *Fire of True Life*, it cannot be present when one experiences Samadhi. For there remains only the reflected Light, when one is returning to the 'human' existence, that is, when Samadhi is finished for us. In this *reflected* light attempts have been made to solve some problems, and the following paragraphs are one of the attempts made in this direction.

* * * *

The foremost factor of the illimitable bliss of Samadhi can be considered as absolute freedom and disinterest in the world left far below and apart from us. Such conceptions as body, earthly life, conditions, physical ties, desires and strivings are now unknown, forgotten, dissolved in the *Orb of Full Light*.

No shadow or regret, no remembrance, either good or sad, exist any more. One ceases to be what before was called the *Man*. For now this term means nothing more than all the limitations connected with the state of the incarnate as well as that of the unincarnate human being. Here this being is transcended. Just as our childhood is transcended in our adult age, and cannot be actual or lived again.

Any name is incompatible with us when we are in Samadhi. The *Light* opens everything to us, without any effort, for no effort exists where there is no more matter. All can be known and at the same moment forgotten for ever in the timeless spiritual realm. From the height of Samadhi everything which has a form seems to be like the shadow of some non-existent world. It is impossible to describe how it finds justification in the consciousness, which itself has evolved from the most primitive state, in which there was no knowledge, or even suggestion of the exalted experiences, which one is living through now. Perhaps it is because only that *Now* exists, without any past or future and all the conceptions of the human mind connected with them.

Normally, we live on the narrow edge between the past and the future, the present being only that thin line of separation. This precarious but compulsory state is due to the properties of the mind.

Now the malefactor becomes an obsolete and far-off unreal shadow, and the 'narrow edge' develops into the all-time-present Now.

The transcendental beauty of this Now is too great for us to find enough words to glorify it. Vain attempt!

While the mind in the mortal body fearfully receded before the immense conception of *eternity*, in Samadhi there are no longer any bonds, and everything is in its own true light. This 'everything' is immense as the Whole, but at the same time it is also tinier than the smallest imaginable thing, like an electron in the physics created by the mind.

In Samadhi alone, the conception of the Supreme Being, called by men—God is fully realized. It happens only because the Unity is realized. The *One Supreme Being is the All*, including the temporarily reintegrated consciousness of man experiencing Samadhi, who, however, is not a 'man' any more.

'*To see God is to be God*,' said one of Those who are eternally in the realm of ultimate Truth, which is God Himself.

It comes to mind, that God can be realized only because the Oneness has been realized, these conditions are interdependent. Who can exist apart from the *One*? Even the mind cannot accept such nonsense and this is quite clear in Samadhi.

What place has humanity, remaining below the level of Superconsciousness, as seen from that height? It must be understood that as no form can be perceived in the spiritual realm of Kevala, nothing can be remembered or seen from the manifested world, including the planet called earth and its dwellers. Some might think that such a 'separation' means loneliness. It would be if consciousness, not sufficiently developed to realize the *Absolute Oneness*, could have access to Samadhi. What is humanity and the multiplicity of other cosmic bodies and their visible or invisible dwellers? Only fragments of the *White Light*, broken up by the prism of duality—*I and Non-I*. There is not, and cannot be any perfection in changeable forms, 'for *perfection* does not need any *change*.' (*In Days of Great Peace*, page 185.)

The cardinal condition of the Kevala is that the one experiencing it has no interest in anything apart from that *Orb of Light*. He cannot conceive of anything higher than the state in which he then dwells, and he intuitively knows, that there cannot be anything beyond it. In this attitude lies the great difficulty of translating into the language of the mind, the reflections of the *Light* in the mind, immediately after our return from Samadhi. This attitude justifies the famous saying:

'*Vanitas Vanitatum et Omnia Vanitas.*'

When you reach Kevala, you experimentally *know* the truth of this proverb and then how could you be interested in such a vanity of vanities? Meditate about this now and perhaps the *Truth* in you might be resuscitated under the influence of *its* reflection in words.

A question was once asked: what remains of one's former loves, and if the Reintegrated Sons of humanity, that is, the spiritual Masters, who lead us to Samadhi, can be perceived in it? No direct answer can be given to this problem, if we are not to depart from truth. All that can be said is that *nothing is* lost from the realm of the Real in Samadhi. This means that the *real* Essence—Consciousness present in the Masters and even in as yet undeveloped human beings, is in the *Orb of Oneness*, as it was before we became aware of this fact. I know that *timelessness* and *eternity* taken as reality and not only as abstruse mental conceptions are extremely hard to convey, because of the immensity of the changes in our consciousness necessary for such realization. But even if, with your mind's eye, you try to analyse the fact, that the physical existence, that is, the limitation of perceptions to just the manifested world, necessitates a definite point of view, which is absolutely unacceptable and unreal to the one belonging to the Samadhi-consciousness, then you may understand wherein lies the mysterious key to the true Wisdom, unbound by any conditions.

It is truly stated in the initiatory 'Voice of the Silence', that 'The Self of Matter and the *Self* of Spirit can never meet. One of the twain must disappear; there is no place for both.' May the student realize this and consequently forgive these attempts to express the inexpressible, when he himself reaches the *Orb of Light*.

In a further attempt to convey something more about the state of Samadhi it must be mentioned, that its absoluteness obliterates, among other things, such 'basic', earthly conceptions like: one's age, sex, position, and emotional and mental qualities. In brief, everything that constitutes the personality of man. Accordingly, everything in humanity's existence which has its roots in bodily forms, is *absent* in Samadhi. There is no better word than 'absent'.

Races, states, social conditions, politics, with all their derivatives, and so on, are for ever banned from the *Orb of Full Light*.

You may ask: what then remains? The only answer will be: the *All* remains, existing in eternity, beyond all conditions, the undimmed consciousness of the *Orb*. The insignificance of the realm of forms and bodies is here too crushing to be compared to anything earthly. Every attempt seems to be too crude and meaningless. The language of similes, despite its evident inadequacy, in this case, alone will allow some trace of the idea to be transmitted to the mind.

So, when we are living on a beautiful day in springtime perceiving the majestic grace of Nature's manifestation, we are not thinking about the chemical components of the dew's crystals on the green blades of fresh grass around us, or about the type of energy enclosed in the warming rays of the life-giving sun. Then we accept things as they *are*. We are only aware of them, and this makes us happy at the time.

Hence, in Samadhi, the consciousness cannot be diverted to any lower realms, but—if this ever happens—we are immediately back in the dark valleys of the relative, conditioned existence. Then the Light is lost. We are out of its Orb. As a consolation, there remains an ineffable, indestructible remembrance of It, and the knowledge of *where lies our true fatherland, that last refuge and sure harbour, in which we are bound to take the final rest after eons of stormy travelling through the ocean of relativity (called 'life' in ignorance) here below.* Perhaps I should not make this attempt to convey something which cannot be understood by the mind, for the true state in which all the aforesaid can be realized, depends upon the stopping of thinking by a conscious effort. Only then one sees the incomparable sublimity and simplicity of Truth-Life, no longer shrouded by thoughts and words. This hint shows the Path.

Another reflection from the Orb may be the absence of what we call 'numerical conceptions' in Samadhi. No such conception dares to find its way into the Reintegrated Superconsciousness. It means that the calculating processes, together with all the others which belong to the mind, are left behind before the Orb has been entered. How difficult it seems to us, to throw out from our present 'normal' consciousness even one attribute such as 'numerical conceptions'.

But the attentive student would agree with this, even if only in meditation. If in Samadhi there is no duality, then the figures 'one', 'two' cannot touch our awareness, so how could the next ones, that is 'three', four', and so on, be perceived?

Here also lies a means which can help us to distinguish Samadhi from the various and innumerable kinds of visions and ecstasies. In the astro-mental realm, in which they manifest themselves, the division into units and numbers still exists, although somewhat differently to that in the mental world. It is like a process of counting in higher dimensions, formulated by some mathematicians in their efforts to embrace, with the mind, what lies beyond it. Units vary in different worlds. It is like the units of the two-dimensional world, which are different to those of the three-dimensional one. But in Samadhi there are no divisions or limitations, therefore all material standards mentioned cannot find any place in it.

The precursors of the 'numberless' life are the different states of mind, which arise during the time of practical study of concentration. I am speaking here about the more or less perfect stillness of the thinking principle, *imposed* (not accidentally obtained) by our own effort of will. In the higher degrees of concentration connected with separation from the senses (foremostly from sight, hearing and touch), one is gazing into absolute 'emptiness', where duality, and with it numerical calculations seem to have become discarded. Simply, you cannot say one, two, or three, and so on.

The conception of death is obliterated in Kevala. Moreover, when returning to the physical consciousness, because of the impossibility to endure the 'high flight' any longer, man often feels acute disgust at dwelling again in the fleshly case. Some have wanted to die rather than to descend again into that, which the inspired and unique Sankaracharya truly calls: 'This gross body . . . made up of skin, flesh, blood, nerves, fat, marrow and bones and . . . filth.'

But the Masters say that this should be avoided. The fact that man is unable at the time to develop his Kevala into eternal Sahaja is the best proof that nothing which is premature is permanent. And death does not add anything to man's qualities, so it cannot be any remedy in this case.

The necessity to live again in the physical or other form does not destroy the power of spiritual enlightenment in Samadhi. The *Orb* is never forgotten. An occultist truly said:

> 'Whoever has once felt the Spirit of the Highest, cannot confuse It with anything else, forget It, or deny Its existence. O world, if thou would refuse to recognize Its existence with a unanimous voice, I would abandon thee and still preserve my faith.'

Another occultist (P. Sédir) said, that the Light is so close to us, that it is truly amazing, that men do not find It. This might happen just *because they do not look.*

For those who retain religious beliefs, the attainment of Kevala Samadhi might mean their paradise. In the visions of St John the Evangelist—apart from purely mental images, which presented to him clichés of the future in the astro-mental light —there are also some higher impressions, about which he 'was forbidden to write', that is, to translate them into human language. This inspired Apostle also often speaks about 'things which no human eye could see or ear hear'. Supposedly, these could be manifestations of the formless Samadhi.

When returning from Samadhi, man is seldom able to retain his exoteric religious conceptions for the future. He has seen too much of Truth to be able to classify It into the categories of popular religions.

Nevertheless, he will have still greater love and admiration for the Great Sons of humanity, who show us the Path leading to spiritual reintegration.

Moreover, he will surely feel, that it is because of their invisible assistance that he was granted the step ahead, by being allowed to merge in the Eternal Light of pure consciousness.

* * * *

We know that physically, man is almost nothing, a bit of dust on a small planet, lost among infinite distances and the innumerable galaxies of the universe, which are accessible to the senses. But, in Samadhi, everything is embraced by our consciousness, which then possesses the attribute of omnipresence and omniscience. How insignificant man is as he is seen on the earth, and how great he is when he return to his eternal fatherland—the Spirit!

* * * *

We will conclude this attempt to describe things which are beyond all speech. The final advice is: no matter what the cost, toil or effort, do not forget that the Path exists, that the Aim is attainable and that It is beyond all you can imagine or conceive of now; that any price paid for its attainment seems to be insignificant when it is reached; that this is the final liberation from slavery in the bonds of matter and the suffering connected with it.

Its attainment is the supreme service and good that you can render to your brethren struggling in the chains of Maya.

> 'Joy unto ye, O Men of Earth.
> A pilgrim hath returned back "from the other shore".
> A new Saviour is born.'
>
> (From *The Voice of the Silence*)

Be welcome in the realm of Light, and on entering It assist to pour It into the darkness of this age.

> 'The dew is on the lotus!—Rise, Great Sun!
> And lift my leaf and mix me with the wave
> Om mani padme hum, the sunrise comes!
> The dewdrop slips into the shining sea!'
>
> (Sir Edwin Arnold's—*The Light of Asia*)

THE END

Bibliography

Arundale, Dr G., *Nirvana*

Augustine, St, *Confessions*

Besant, Dr Annie, *A Study in Consciousness*

Brandler-Pracht, Dr, *Geistige Erziehung*

James, William, *The Varieties of Religious Experience*

Kempis, Thomas à, *Imitation of Christ*

Maharshi, Sri Ramana, *Forty Verses*

Maharshi, Sri Ramana, *Maharshi's Gospel* (Books I and II)

Maharshi, Sri Ramana, *Self-Inquiry*

Maharshi, Sri Ramana, *Spiritual Instruction*

Maharshi, Sri Ramana, *Truth Revealed*

Maharshi, Sri Ramana, *Who Am I?*

Plato, *Dialogue: Crito*

Plotinus, *Enneades*

Ribhu Gita, From the Hindu Scriptures

Sadhu, Mouni, *Concentration*

Sadhu, Mouni, *In Days of Great Peace*

Sadhu, Mouni, *The Tarot, a Contemporary Course of Hermetic Occultism*

Sankaracharya, *Viveka Chudamani (The Crest Jewel of Wisdom)*

Sarma, Sri Lakshmana, *Maha Yoga*

Sédir, Paul, *Initiations*

Sédir, Paul, *L'Energie Ascetique*

Sédir, Paul, *Le Royaume de Dieu*

Sédir, Paul, *Le Sacrifice*

Sédir, Paul, *Le Sermon sur la Montagne*

Sédir, Paul, *Les Forces Mystiques et la Conduite de la Vie*

Sédir, Paul, *Les Sept Jardins Mystiques*

Sédir, Paul, *Quelques Amis de Dieu*

Shastri, Dr Hari Prasad, translator, *Ashtavakra Gita*